Geoffrey Ashe

King Arthur

The dream of a golden age

with 120 illustrations, 15 in color

Thames and Hudson

ART AND IMAGINATION

© 1990 Thames and Hudson Ltd, London

First published in the United States in 1990 by
Thames and Hudson Inc., 500 Fifth Avenue,
New York, New York 10110

Library of Congress Catalog Card Number
89–51587

Printed and bound in Singapore by C.S Graphics Ltd

Contents

. . . Indeed, by this time, Britain had reached such a standard of sophistication that it excelled all other kingdoms in its general affluence, the richness of its decorations, and the courteous behaviour of its inhabitants. Every knight in the country who was in any way famed for his bravery wore livery and arms showing his own distinctive colour; and women of fashion often displayed the same colours. They scorned to give their love to any man who had not proved himself three times in battle. In this way the womenfolk became chaste and more virtuous and for their love the knights were ever more daring.

Geoffrey of Monmouth on the reign of Arthur
(translation by Lewis Thorpe)

The dream of a golden age
The story

Arthur, as a quasi-historical king, is the creation of one writer. Geoffrey of Monmouth was a cleric, of Welsh or possibly Breton descent. Little is known about him beyond the fact that he was teaching at Oxford between 1129 and 1151. Towards 1138 he produced a Latin work misleadingly titled *Historia Regum Britanniae*, The History of the Kings of Britain. He may have had sources unknown to us, as well as some that we do know, but his own imagination was predominant. The so-called *History* which it shaped was one of the most important books of the Middle Ages.

It begins in the twelfth century BC after the fall of Troy, with a wandering Trojan prince named Brutus, who, according to a legend older than Geoffrey, conducted a party of Trojans to this island. Geoffrey presents Brutus and his companions as the original Britons. He continues through a long series of kings and queens. A few are historical. A few more may be. Others have their origin in Celtic mythology. Others are persons taken from early Welsh genealogies and blithely depicted as ancient monarchs.

After the phase of Roman rule, reduced to a protectorate with the royal line going on, Geoffrey moves towards the Arthurian climax. Britain, parted from the Empire early in the fifth century AD, falls into the power of an unscrupulous noble called Vortigern, who usurps the crown and drives two rightful princes abroad. Heathen Saxons arrive from across the North Sea, led by the brothers Hengist and Horsa, and Vortigern makes a disastrous treaty with them, allowing them and further Saxons to settle in Britain as auxiliary troops. Many more pour into the country, get out of hand, massacre Vortigern's lords, and overrun and devastate much of Britain. Vortigern flees to Wales, where he meets the young seer Merlin, who performs marvellous feats and foretells a king who will save Britain, but also foretells that before then the princes will return and Vortigern will be slain. This duly happens. The elder prince, Aurelius Ambrosius, becomes king and wins a victory over the Saxons, only to be poisoned by one of them after a short reign. His brother Uther (called the Pendragon or 'Foremost Leader') succeeds him, and continues to contain the heathen, though still without decisive success. Both brothers have kept in touch with Merlin, whom they respect for his gift of prophecy and his secret arts.

At Easter, Geoffrey tells us, King Uther held a banquet in London. Among the guests were Gorlois, Duke of Cornwall, and his lovely wife Ygerna. Uther was filled with violent and obvious desire for her. Gorlois withdrew from the court without asking leave and went back to Cornwall with his wife. Uther took this act as an insult, and followed with an army to ravage the ducal lands. Gorlois lodged Ygerna in his castle of Tintagel, on a rocky headland approachable only by a narrow isthmus, in the belief that the King could not reach her there. Then he marched off to meet the royal forces. Unfortunately for him, Merlin was with them. By his arts he transformed Uther into a replica of the Duke, enabling him to pass the guards at Tintagel, who assumed him to be their master returning. Thus he spent a night with Ygerna and begot Arthur, destined to be the national deliverer whom Merlin had prophesied. Gorlois had fallen in battle, so Uther could revert to his real appearance and make Ygerna his queen.

Arthur succeeded to the throne while still very young, but soon showed genius as a leader, routing the Saxons and confining them to a small area. Throughout his reign they remained subject to him and harmless. He

Arthur's coronation, in the medieval style established by Geoffrey of Monmouth. No one knows what the ritual would have been when he conceives Arthur as reigning, but he draws on the ceremonial of his own time for descriptions. (Manuscript illustration, Italian, 14th c.)

conquered the Picts and Scots, who had also been causing trouble; sailed across and conquered the Irish, who had been helping them; and then sailed north and conquered Iceland. Meanwhile he had married Guinevere, a lady of Roman descent. With her as queen, he reigned in peace and prosperity for twelve years, beloved of all the Britons. During this time he founded an order of knighthood, enrolling men of distinction from foreign lands as well as his own.

He added Norway and Denmark to his domains. Gaul, across the Channel, was still shakily in Roman hands. Arthur conquered a large part of it, and spent several years, during a second period of peace, organizing his conquests. He appointed two of his principal knights, Kay and Bedivere, as continental viceroys. When fully satisfied with the state of his empire, he held court at the former Roman town of Caerleon in Gwent, receiving the homage of kings, nobles and prelates. During the splendid ceremonies, ambassadors from Rome arrived, demanding that he pay tribute as in times past and restore his conquests. Arthur retorted by leading another army across the Channel, leaving his nephew Mordred in charge at home, jointly with the Queen. He defeated the imperial forces and entered Burgundy, but news was brought that Mordred had proclaimed himself king, persuaded Guinevere to live in adultery with him, and made a deal with the Saxons, allotting them large tracts of land in return for military support. Arthur went back to Britain and crushed the traitor by the River Camel in Cornwall. But he was grievously wounded himself, and handed over the crown to a cousin, Constantine. Then he was 'carried off to the Isle of Avalon so that his wounds might be attended to'. Of his final fate, nothing is said.

When is this supposed to have happened? Geoffrey supplies a few calibrations with known history. Vortigern makes his main agreement with Hengist at the time of a visitation by two Gallic bishops, Germanus and Lupus, and this is a real event that took place in 429. During Arthur's Gallic campaigning there are three allusions to an emperor Leo, and he has to be Leo I, who reigned from 457 to 474. On this basis, Arthur's reign can be squared with what is said or implied about the previous kings and the family relationships. Geoffrey says also that he departed to Avalon in 542, a year incompatible with almost everything up to then. However, a study of known types of error in early documents suggests that what we have here could be a misguided 'correction' of a date within Leo's reign.

Geoffrey is not a historian and can never be relied on for facts. On the other hand, once he has left his pre-Roman world behind, he is seldom or never inventing out of nothing at all. He uses older materials as the ingredients of his fiction. While Arthur as portrayed is impossible, he does have antecedents. To assess his career in literature, to grasp what his story is about and account for its spell, those antecedents need to be looked at.

Where the story came from

Behind Geoffrey's Arthur is a body of tradition, some of it written, most of it (so far as we know) oral. Transmitted chiefly by the Welsh, it was drawn not only from Wales itself but from areas with people of kindred stock: from Strathclyde, Cumbria, Cornwall, Brittany. It related to Britain on the eve of its severance from the Roman Empire and in the century or two after that. The Welsh and their kinsfolk were descendants of Celtic Britons who inhabited the country under the Empire. They, or their upper social strata at least, had received imperial culture and Christianity. Their Romanization survived in some degree after the break with Rome.

That break occurred, for practical purposes, about the year 410. Power began slipping into the hands of chiefs and officials who founded what became regional dynasties. Presently the British Celts had a ruler comparable to the high kings of the Irish Celts, who claimed to be supreme over lesser rulers. This was the man whom Geoffrey calls Vortigern. In the fifth-century context 'Vortigern' is a title or designation, rather than a proper name. Its meaning is 'over-chief', in effect, 'high king'.

The Britons, in their exposed position, had been subject for many years to foreign raiding: by Irish from the west, by Picts from what is now Scotland, and by Saxons, ancestors of the English, from across the North Sea. The imperial forces had found it harder and harder to cope with them, and when those forces had gone, Britain's rulers faced a serious problem. Shortly before the end of the Roman period, a few Saxons had made their homes in the island on a peaceful basis, apparently with permission as *foederati*, barbarians allotted land and maintenance in return for keeping order and repelling other barbarians. This arrangement was seen as a solution. From about the 420s on, the number of auxiliaries rose sharply. Still known collectively as Saxons, they comprised Saxons proper, Angles, Jutes, and minor groupings from the same continental Germanic background.

Vortigern doubtless authorized these settlements, or some of them. The Welsh blamed him in retrospect for the whole process. Many more Saxons entered Britain, more than the Britons could maintain. Towards the middle of the fifth century they revolted, raiding and pillaging far and wide, probably not in one catastrophic surge, but piecemeal over a decade or more.

Finally they ceased raiding and remained for a while within their authorized enclaves. What happened next forms the basis of the Arthurian legend. Events in Britain followed a unique course. Barbarians had moved into many parts of the Empire. But here, as nowhere else, a provincial people had become *de facto* self-governing before they moved in. And here, as nowhere else, a provincial people cared enough to fight back. A counter-offensive took shape under a leader named Ambrosius Aurelianus, the original of Geoffrey's Aurelius Ambrosius. A to-and-fro warfare continued for years in parts of Britain, and the Britons managed, in places, to stabilize the position. Archaeology shows that they reoccupied many hill-forts of the pre-Roman Iron Age, sometimes only as places of refuge, but sometimes as military bases and centres of government.

Towards the year 500, a British victory at an unidentified Mount Badon, perhaps one of the refurbished hill-forts, brought a generation or two of relative peace and equilibrium. Political cohesion, however, had gone, and the Empire itself had perished in the west. Britain's Roman-founded towns were sunk in decay. The British language was beginning to disintegrate, with the emergence of Welsh and other regional variants not far off. The petty kings quarrelled among themselves and pursued their own ends. Meanwhile the balance of population tilted against them, and few of them took any measures to stop another Saxon advance.

The Britons' gradual collapse in the face of that advance turned most of the country into England, Angle-land. But they handed down heroic legends that were preserved and improved by the people of their stock in the north, Wales, Cornwall, Brittany. The 'original Arthur' (to use a convenient term) is embedded in this traditional matter, not as the colossus that Geoffrey makes him, but as a successful war-leader of the Britons and a paramount figure during one of their phases of ascendancy.

Early Welsh allusions to him unfortunately spread his career over an impossible time-range, from the middle of the fifth century to the middle of the sixth. This Arthur of the Welsh may be a composite of several men, champions of resistance at different times. Or there may indeed have been an 'original Arthur', one only, whose *floruit* was extended because the actions of heirs or followers after his death were attributed by bards to him personally. Such an original would fit best into the second half of the fifth century, perhaps as a nominal successor of Vortigern, with Ambrosius as a general in his service. 'Arthur' is a Welsh form of the Roman name Artorius. It suggests a Briton born when the country was still close to the imperial civilization. Records of several Arthurs during the later sixth century imply that someone called Arthur had by then become a national hero, after whom boys were named.

Geoffrey's pseudo-biography is not pure fancy but a mélange, though his imagination inflates and alters everything it takes hold of. Here as elsewhere he does make use of history, including, it seems, some account of an actual expedition to Gaul in 468–70, by a British king who may be the original Arthur so far as anyone was. He has read Welsh notes on Arthur's wars and final demise, listing battles against the Angles in Lincolnshire and against Picts in alliance with them in Scotland. By picking on Tintagel for Uther's encounter with Arthur's mother he shows awareness of the fact, rediscovered only by archaeology, that Tintagel was a major stronghold at about the right time. He knows also that bards and story-tellers mythified Arthur into a saga hero, a warrior prince with a host of adventurous companions, fighting giants and monsters. From that milieu he adopts a giant or two, but he is more concerned with the companions, basing Arthur's knights on them and taking over a few directly, such as Cei and Bedwyr, who become Kay and Bedivere.

So far as can be judged, the saga absorbed an appreciable amount of pre-Christian mythology. Welsh tales on other themes, in the collection known as the *Mabinogion*, certainly did. Celtic Christians in Britain and Ireland had a hospitable attitude to the former gods and goddesses. Christians in these lands were willing to continue believing in them. Of course, they could no longer be divine, but they could survive in thinly disguised myths, thinly disguised themselves as kings and queens and enchanters and fairy-folk. The Irish went further than the Welsh, but the difference was one of degree merely.

Several Arthurian characters seem to have a pagan background. One who raises immediate questions is Merlin, who foretells Arthur and in a sense creates him. He is a fusion by Geoffrey of two or even three characters into a new figure. If an 'original Merlin' is wanted, he is a British noble of the late sixth century, who was reputedly driven out of his mind at a battle in Cumbria and wandered through southern Scotland uttering prophecies, blessed or cursed with second-sight. While northern records call him Lailoken, Welsh poems give him a more dignified air and call him Myrddin, a sobriquet implying a link with Carmarthen. He is credited with foretelling a Celtic resurgence.

Geoffrey at first knew his name or alias, but not much more. Before he completed the *History* he published some alleged prophecies of the seer, Latinizing 'Myrddin' after his own fashion. Wanting to build them into the *History*, he had to bring in 'Merlin' to utter them. Welsh legend furnished him with a tale of a young seer with no human father (being begotten, Geoffrey inferred, by a spirit or incubus), whose feats confounded Vortigern. Geoffrey put this episode in the *History*, making out that the legendary youth *was* Merlin and allotting the prophecies to him. The date, however, was more than a hundred years out. Later he learned more about the northerner, and wrote a narrative poem, the *Vita Merlini*, Life of Merlin, in which he tried to fudge dates and details to make the two identical.

There is more to it than this, though the rest is obscure. In one or two Welsh poems, 'Myrddin' has been construed as meaning a spirit of inspiration rather than an individual. A man such as Lailoken, deemed to have prophetic powers, may therefore have been a Myrddin-man or simply a Myrddin. There may be a recollection here of some prehistoric god, a god of inspiration. Geoffrey's own story hints that a superhuman being may have gone into the making of his Merlin. The enchanter is responsible for Stonehenge, which was formerly in Ireland, but which he dismantles and reassembles on Salisbury Plain.

To revert to Arthur, Geoffrey established him as a splendid monarch and victorious conqueror. The *History* was widely read, and believed. Geoffrey's purpose in writing was probably quite limited. He wanted to show that his Celtic kinsfolk, so sadly reduced by English power, had a glorious ancestry and, according to Merlin, an encouraging future. In the outcome, however, he did much more. He gave a strong impetus to a discovery of Celtic mythology by the English and French, and supplied a quasi-historical frame into which it could be fitted, both as it came from his own hands and as it was spread from other sources, notably by Breton minstrels.

The visionary kingdom

Arthurian legend takes on its most familiar guise in romances written during the late twelfth century and the thirteenth. These created the elaborate montage which Arthur's name now evokes: the King himself, a resplendent medieval sovereign; Guinevere, his fair and passionate queen; Merlin, the royal magician; Camelot, the royal city; the Round Table knighthood, vowed to high ideals; the tragic love-stories of Lancelot and Guinevere, Tristan and Isolde; the sacred mystery of the Grail Quest.

Medieval romancers recognized three main sources of material. The Matter of Rome meant classical antiquity. The Matter of France meant Charlemagne, Roland, and the rest of the Frankish emperor's peers, around the year 800. The Matter of Britain meant chiefly Arthur and his court. This eclipsed the others in popularity and spread throughout western Christendom.

At first most of the authors were French, using the language spoken by their public on both sides of the Channel. Wace, a poetic adapter of Geoffrey's *History*, was followed by Chrétien de Troyes with elegant verse tales introducing new characters, notably Lancelot. A series of French romances in prose established what afterwards remained the approved pattern. However, there was no lasting French monopoly. The German poet Wolfram von Eschenbach contributed *Parzival*, the inspiration of Wagner's opera, and England produced epics and tales of which the best is *Sir Gawain and the Green Knight*. Other nations made their own additions. In the end it was an English author, Sir Thomas Malory, who gave the medieval legend such unity as it ever acquired. His monumental work, printed by Caxton in a revised form as the *Morte d'Arthur*, was finished in 1469 and is a remodelling of earlier French and English materials.

All the romances exhibit a medieval practice, already plain in Geoffrey but now carried further, which almost disconnects the literature from whatever facts underlie it. They update. Medieval authors handling a story from olden times make no attempt at authenticity. They put virtually everything in terms of contemporary experience and interests. Government, architecture, clothing, weaponry, sports, geography, social customs, are all medieval. That is why Arthur's fifth-century companions become knights in armour, why hill-forts become castles, why simple churches become cathedrals, why a Celtic society becomes a courtly one. The romancers' enhanced Arthurian Britain absorbs the previous elements, real and fictitious, but transfigures them in a new creation: a chivalric Utopia with Arthur presiding.

He is presently enrolled in a standard constellation of heroes, the Nine Worthies. Three were Jewish: Joshua, David, and Judas Maccabaeus. Three were pagan: Hector, Alexander, and Julius Caesar. Three were Christian: Arthur himself, Charlemagne, and Godfrey of Bouillon, the leader of the First Crusade.

Arthur's kingdom has a magical aspect. This is due in part to fragments of pre-Christian mythology, drifting into it from the Celtic past. It is due more conspicuously to the promotion of Merlin. Geoffrey's Merlin contrives Arthur's birth and is still alive after his passing, but is never portrayed actually meeting him. Later authors found the character too alluring to leave alone. His cryptic prophecies were taken seriously and interpreted. His strange origin as the son of an incubus was improved. The story now was that a devil begot him, to produce a man having paranormal gifts who would use them against Christianity. The mother's piety thwarted this intention, and while her son had the paranormal gifts, he was willing to employ them constructively.

Romancers make Merlin the sponsor of the whole Arthurian regime, preparing the way for it, enthroning the young King, equipping him by magical means, using prophetic powers to advise him. Merlin not only contrives Arthur's birth but provides for his fostering in a distant place, to keep him safe in an interregnum following Uther's death, till the time is ripe for him to emerge. He makes the Round Table which will be central to Arthur's court. When Arthur is old enough to take charge, Merlin proves his right by the test of the sword driven into the stone, which only Britain's true sovereign can extract. He aids the King in his struggles against resentful challengers, and, when the sword drawn from the stone is broken, arranges for him to receive Excalibur.

In Geoffrey's *History* Arthur has a sword Caliburn, forged by fairy-folk, and in romance the hint is developed. The slightly re-named and wonderful Excalibur is a gift from the Lady of the Lake. She is perhaps, in her origins, a priestess. Her sacred pool, or an enchanted space below, is the home of a group of damsels under her headship, and when a Lady dies, one of the damsels succeeds her. Lancelot is called Lancelot of the Lake because the current Lady took him away as a child and brought him up. Merlin is on friendly terms with the Lake community, and one of the damsels is his undoing.

His relationship with the King is an unusual conception. European legend has nothing else quite like it. A parallel of sorts is the role of Krishna in the *Mahabharata*. Krishna is divine, an avatar of the supreme god Vishnu. In the Hindu epic he befriends Yudhishthir, the Pandava king who is dispossessed by his cousins. When Yudhishthir moves to reclaim his rights, and war breaks out, Krishna joins him as a non-combatant adviser. In several crises of the war he saves the situation by ruses which – it must be confessed – leave an unpleasant taste, however worthy the object. He is a trickster, therefore liable to comparison with Merlin, and the comparison, humanly speaking, is sometimes in Merlin's favour.

The golden age

Throughout western Europe, the Arthurian fashion produced literature in the major languages and art in the major countries. There were several reasons for the flowering. The Crusades played a significant part. The contact of western Europe with the civilized east promoted new interests and refinements. The revival of Christian energy, and intense concern with the Holy Land, gave a fresh life to religious consciousness and helped to inspire the Arthurian mythos of the Grail. The long absences of nobles meant that their wives, back in the castle, assumed more responsibility. While the real power-relation between the sexes was little altered, feminine tastes in such fields as entertainment began to carry weight; and Arthurian romances had a great deal to offer here, far more than the old masculine epics such as the *Song of Roland*. They had a great deal to offer in a broader sense. They had something for everybody – war, tournaments, adventures, quests, magic, love, religion, heraldry. The rival Matters could not compete.

Yet as we stand back and contemplate all this, it is clear that it can apply only to the vogue in a particular period, the Middle Ages. It cannot explain the legend's enduring fascination, its ability to keep appearing in different guises, fading and returning, from Welsh story-tellers before Geoffrey right through to twentieth-century novelists whose sales bear witness. Arthur stands for something deep-seated, and the chivalric Utopia is only one of the outward forms he gives it: he has the power to generate others. He bestows a British shape on the perennial dream of a long-ago, long-lost golden age. This is a constant that runs as a haunting undercurrent through different versions.

The golden age is a widespread conception. In ancient China, the first phase of the Chou dynasty, reigning from about 1100 BC, was looked back upon as an era of social harmony and wise government, conducted by moral force, not coercion. Confucius characterized the lost Chou rightness as *Tao*, the Way, meaning the Way of the Former Kings, and a central aim of his teaching was to revive it.

In Hinduism the picture is more cosmic and complex. The world passes through a series of yugas or aeons, and the first, the Krita, is the best. During the Krita Yuga, rulers were just and public-spirited, priests were holy, the different social orders did their duty. But that was many thousands of years ago. Three more yugas ensued, each one shorter and worse, and we are now in the last, the Kali Yuga, which will go on deteriorating till divine intervention halts the process.

Greece also had a series of ages. The standard account is given by the poet Hesiod in the eighth century BC. First, he says, came the age of 'golden' people. This is where the epithet 'golden' makes its appearance. It was an era of gods-before-the-gods, the primordial beings known as Titans, their chief being Cronus, whom the Romans later called Saturn. The golden people lived happily without effort on the fruits of the earth, had no diseases and never grew old. Death held no terrors for them, and they still live on in the world as benign spirits, but not as a visible human race.

They were succeeded by 'silver' people, who were comparatively dull but peaceful, and matriarchally ruled. Cronus's son Zeus, however, exiled and banished him. The senior deity ended up in a far-away west, an Elysium across the ocean, where something of his golden age lingered with him. Meanwhile Zeus had wiped out the silver race, and replaced it with violent people who ate meat and used tools and weapons of bronze. (We are coming into contact here with archaeological fact and the real Bronze Age.) Through coupling with gods, their women produced a nobler bronze stock, the heroes who sailed in Argo and fought at Troy. The best of them live on with Cronus in his western Elysium. None are to be found any more in the familiar world. Their base successors were 'iron' men. For Hesiod his own time is the iron age, which, like the Kali Yuga, is the worst.

Hesiod looks ahead only to further worsening and perhaps extinction. Transferred to the Roman milieu, the scheme is less gloomy and takes a surprising turn. Humanity has indeed lost the age of Cronus, the *Saturnia regna*; but Virgil, as poet-laureate to Augustus Caesar, declares not only that it can be reborn but that Augustus is actually effecting this. The peace, good government, and prosperity of his reign embody the same golden qualities. Virgilian optimism could not last, yet centuries later, in the Empire's decline, hopes persisted for a ruler who would at least recover its best days. A golden age of sorts might still be brought back by a *Restitutor Orbis* or World-Restorer, and almost to the very end in the west, ephemeral emperors were still being hailed as such. Arthur himself, as portrayed by Geoffrey, seems to echo this yearning and to become briefly a *Restitutor* within the limits of his ex-Roman Britain.

Plainly the golden age is a potent theme. There are many more instances. It need not be located far back in a mythical prehistory. For Confucius the early Chou era was a matter of four or five centuries before his own birth. The Welsh story-tellers who created their Arthurian world, their golden age, before Geoffrey and the romancers, were thinking of a time at much the same distance from themselves: the time of the Britons' unique rally against the barbarians, and their holding their own, in a phase of glory which Arthur had come to symbolize, thanks to bards and occasional clerics who had transmitted his fame. The Welsh image survives in one complete tale, though we have sketches and summaries of others now lost. *Culhwch and Olwen* is a wild, colourful story with a good deal of ruthlessness and black humour. Here the age of Arthur is essentially a heroic age, an age of warriors and marvels, of monsters and giants and superhuman feats. Arthur is the chief prince of Britain, the Island of the Mighty, and most Britons of legendary standing are at his court, more than two hundred of them, often in defiance of chronology.

When Geoffrey takes up the subject, making Arthur a quasi-historical monarch and a kind of Messiah, he combines Welsh tradition with genuine history, and expands both on a lavish scale. But with Geoffrey we encounter the medieval updating. While he too describes Arthur's court, he does it in thoroughly twelfth-century terms. Also he does it at greater length, and in more detail, than the mere updating would require. He is giving substance to the Arthurian golden age as he imagines it himself, and in a form acceptable to his readers. We are not told much about the condition of the populace, but Geoffrey assures us that the King's generosity and other fine qualities endeared him to all. The rest of the literature assumes the justice and prosperity of his reign, or most of it.

After Geoffrey comes the chivalric Utopia of the romancers, evoked first by Chrétien de Troyes. In their hands the golden age is entirely medieval or ideal-medieval, and the historical roots still visible in Geoffrey have almost vanished. Part of his story that has a tenuous connection with fact, Arthur's Gallic warfare, survives in an English epic known as the *Alliterative Morte Arthure*. When Malory carries out his vast rehandling, he uses this epic as well as the French romances, and it is instructive to see what he does with it. Geoffrey and the *Alliterative Morte* portray the King's principal campaign against Rome as coming at the end of his reign, and occasioning his downfall. Malory shifts it many years back. His Arthur triumphs and returns, and a very long peace ensues, in which numerous things happen. Malory's purpose is clear. He is creating a space, more firmly defined than in previous versions, for the golden age to flourish in.

Beyond the Middle Ages, the next full treatment is Tennyson's. In his *Idylls of the King* he follows Malory, but not slavishly, and changes the atmosphere. As a conscientious laureate, devoted to the Queen and the memory of her Consort, he recasts the legend in a mould of Victorian values. Once again Arthur presides over a golden age. But now it has that quality because it is spiritually inspired, with high ideals mastering the baser nature, the animal element in humanity. More is said about Christian love and marriage, as symbolizing the mastery, and the evils that undermine the kingdom have an allegorical quality, 'shadowing Sense at war with Soul'.

In the twentieth century, T.H. White's tetralogy *The Once and Future King* is again Malory-based. But White develops the golden-age aspect in his own style, a modern one, stressing ideals like peace and internationalism. In the upshot, it is more a matter of hope than of achievement, but the King is justified by his good intentions.

After White a series of novelists, such as Rosemary Sutcliff, Mary Stewart and Persia Woolley, have approached the legend from a new angle. Their inspiration has come from serious research into Post-Roman Britain by archaeologists and historians. By-passing the romance tradition, they have based historical novels and fantasies on the original Arthur and his country as they actually were . . . or may have been. Poets, notably Charles Williams and John Heath-Stubbs, have absorbed similar influences in a lesser degree. Modern writers, aware of the unlikelihood of a real golden age, have nevertheless pictured an Arthurian Britain where people of goodwill, courage and integrity are on top, at least for a while; or where, even in the midst of strife and confusion, great personalities make their mark.

In other media, the musical *Camelot* by Lerner and Loewe draws its inspiration from White and closes with much the same conclusion. Arthur's regime goes down, but for 'one brief shining moment' the vision of a noble society lived, and it remains valid for ever. The film *Excalibur* resembles the novels in emphasizing great individuals rather than an idealized kingdom. It does this in a mixture of periods and imagery intended to take the story outside any kind of history, and convert it into a timeless myth.

The Round Table and Camelot

Arthurian romance in the Middle Ages focuses its golden age on the knighthood of the Round Table. Arthur's order of chivalry is already present in Geoffrey of Monmouth, where the King's enrolment of knights from foreign nations opens the way for the pre-eminence of the foreigner Lancelot, though Lancelot does not appear till Chrétien introduces him. The conception is medieval. Geoffrey is adapting the Welsh tradition that makes Arthur the head of a martial company. He has no actual Round Table. This is mentioned first in Wace's French adaptation of his *History*, produced in 1155. Wace ascribes the Table's shape to a practical motive. By putting all the knights on an equal footing, Arthur prevented quarrels over precedence. But the conception grows more elaborate. Romancers give the Table a pedigree. Merlin made it for Uther, Arthur's father. Its roundness symbolized the round earth and heavens. When Uther died it was acquired by Leodegan, a local ruler. Guinevere was his daughter, and brought the Table to Arthur as a dowry. We are told further that, besides its cosmic symbolism, it was a successor to two previous tables. First came the table of Christ's Last Supper; then, in commemoration of that, a table on which the Grail was kept; then, in commemoration of that, the Round Table of Arthur – so that there was a tangible link between his order of knighthood and the disciples of Christ, between chivalry and religion.

With the literary flowering, attention tends to shift from the King to the knights and ladies around him. The chivalric Utopia is constituted by the vows taken, the ideals prevailing. Arthur's kingdom is a place, theoretically, of justice and honour, fortitude and true love. Many of the adventures of his paladins are set in motion by their duty to right wrongs, succour the distressed, slay monsters, and so forth. Yet most of them are – to put it politely – flawed. Sir Kay, Arthur's seneschal or household manager, is boastful and curmudgeonly. Sir Gawain, though admirable in English tales, is portrayed by the French as untrustworthy and a womanizer, and even English admirers sometimes feel bound to admit his vengefulness. Sir Perceval spends much time being stupid and making costly mistakes. Sir Lancelot, French-born and 'the best knight in the world', becomes the Queen's lover with eventually fatal results. These and others like them are the King's counsellors, responsible for the conduct of the court and, in some cases, for the government of domains of their own. The golden-ness of the golden age does not consist so much in fully realized virtue as in atmosphere and aspiration. Yet it holds up. The King, though by no means unflawed himself, is charismatic enough to keep the atmosphere alive and sustain the aspiration. He has a talent for bringing out the best in others. The summer of his reign is *felt* to be good.

Winchester's Round Table, c. 1300. Eighteen feet across, it is a table-top only, because the legs are lost. The design in green and white segments, giving places for the King and twenty-four knights, was painted in 1522 by order of Henry VIII (hence the Tudor rose) and repainted without change in 1789. (Great Hall, Winchester Castle.)

During the Middle Ages, England's Plantagenet kings took Arthur seriously and sometimes tried to exploit him politically. It is ironic that a Celtic hero, renowned for fighting the ancestors of the English, should have been adopted as a king of England and held to shed ancient lustre on its monarchy; but so he was. Edward I claimed sovereignty over Scotland on the ground that Arthur was sovereign over Scotland. Edward III contemplated refounding the Arthurian knighthood. Monarchs and lords, not only in England, held entertainments called Round Tables at which the guests played Arthurian roles. The Round Table on the wall in Winchester Castle dates from somewhere about 1300, and may have been made for a festivity of this type.

In later works the focus of the golden age is a place, Camelot. There is no contradiction or innovation here, only a shift of emphasis. Camelot is in early romances, primarily as a castle where the Round Table is housed, King Arthur's favourite residence. Around it is a town named after it. A point seldom noticed is that Camelot, as portrayed by the romancers who invented it, is not a national capital. It is purely Arthur's home, the heart of his world. No one else reigns there before or after him. Its character is thus unique. The mystique of Camelot, unlike the mystique of Jerusalem or Rome, is a projection of one mythified person, the golden-age hero. Malory, who sometimes equates it with the old capital Winchester, is therefore misguided. Camelot is a place of the imagination. While it seems to be vaguely in the west, it cannot be located.

The only sense in which a real place could have 'been' Camelot would be as the headquarters of the original Arthur, the starting-point of a tradition that he had such a headquarters. It is in that sense that the claim of Cadbury Castle in Somerset can be entertained. Cadbury is an Iron Age hill-fort south-east of Glastonbury. Associations with Arthur can be proved some centuries back, in a work by the Tudor traveller John Leland, who calls it 'Camalat' outright. Excavation has revealed that it was reoccupied and refurbished about the second half of the fifth century. That happened with other hill-forts, but the size and structure of the Cadbury refortification have no known parallel, in that period, anywhere else in Britain. This was the headquarters of an outstanding ruler, even a 'high king', with great resources of manpower: the original Arthur possibly, or at least an Arthur-figure who could have gone into the making of the legend. The probability of a tradition of some kind is very strong. When Tennyson was planning his *Idylls*, and looking at Arthurian sites in the West Country, Cadbury was one of the sites he looked at. His description of Camelot, though fantasy, fits the topography well enough to suggest that he remembered it.

Love in Arthur's kingdom

In the treatment of sexual relations, as in other respects, Arthurian romances expanded consciousness. During the twelfth century, French troubadours were developing a poetic love-cult. Courtly Love became a literary convention bound up (if on somewhat uneasy terms) with chivalry. Amours were supposed to obey rules. A knight should be utterly devoted to his lady, should idealize and idolize her, should be ready to do or suffer virtually anything for her, even if it put him to shame. If their relationship was correctly conducted, the lady would be domineering, able to throw her lover into the wildest distress, yet, after her fashion, be faithful to him. Any marital commitment she had was a separate matter. One of the rules, in fact, stated that this kind of love could not exist between persons married to each other. In romance it might remain on a footing of adoration; it might be consummated, adulterously if need be; it might end in marriage between the couple, and transition to a love of a different sort.

There is not much evidence for Courtly Love happening in real life. Even as a literary convention it had its limitations. It was explicitly not for the lower orders. The amatory worship of women had little to do with genuine elevation of status, and was sometimes countered, even in romances, by anti-feminist grumblings that the man was likely to regret his involvement. What is special about the Arthurian cycle is that its sense of a heightening of life created two memorable love-stories, the first things of their kind in Europe, which, while reflecting courtly convention, transcended it.

Lancelot, the most splendid of Arthur's knights, is the lover of Queen Guinevere. When he is first introduced, by Chrétien de Troyes, their amour conforms to courtly rules, and the behaviour of both is contrived and off-putting. But as the story evolves, it improves. Richard Harris, who played Arthur in *Camelot*, remarked acutely that this love-triangle has a peculiar interest. Arthur, alone perhaps among literary husbands, has an unfaithful wife without being reduced or made ridiculous. One reason may be that there is more here than medieval fiction. The story has roots in ancient pagan society. A Celtic queen was free and equal, able to rule in her own right and even lead armies, and she could take lovers as the king could take concubines. By the time the tale of Arthur and Guinevere reaches the Middle Ages, society has grown more male-dominated, and the free and equal queen becomes an adulteress. Yet something of her former status remains, and something of her consort's unimpaired dignity.

It is an interesting question whether Guinevere has a mythic aspect, reflecting pagan belief that a queen had a special relationship with a goddess, or even embodied her. 'Guinevere' is the Welsh 'Gwenhwyfar' meaning 'White Phantom' or 'Fay'. There is a strange Welsh allusion to Arthur having three queens called Gwenhwyfar, which has been construed in terms of a Celtic Triple Goddess.

Guinevere's finest medieval development is in Malory. His account of her love-affair is compassionate, sometimes subtle. In his hands Lancelot goes through stages. At first the knight takes a rather anti-feminist line, saying attachment to a woman would hinder his more manly pursuits. He already loves the Queen, but in a distant and proper way. Presently the involvement grows more intense and intimate, till a stage is reached where an angry rejection on her part temporarily unhinges his mind. Towards the end of his work Malory draws a distinction between fidelity and loyalty. Even with the adultery long established, Lancelot can still assure Arthur that Guinevere has been true to him, and, in a deeper sense, she has. She has never failed in her duties, or spoken against him, or acted seditiously, or considered breaking their marriage up. Her earthly love is never debasing, and it enables her to pass to a higher one and die close to sainthood.

The other famous pair, Tristan and Isolde, also carry the love theme beyond convention. Tristan is a nephew of Mark, king of Cornwall under Arthur. His home is in Lyonesse, a country of romance which comes to be

Tristan and Isolde. Scenes from their story were popular in the Middle Ages as decorative motifs on boxes, mirror-backs, cups and pendants. (German ivory casket, c. 1200.)

identified with a sunken land, a mini-Atlantis, located by folklore south and west of Cornwall. He goes to live at the Cornish court. He is sent to Ireland to fetch Isolde, an Irish princess, as a bride for his uncle Mark. On the voyage they accidentally drink a potion and fall irrevocably in love. Isolde marries Mark nevertheless. The lovers spend time together with much difficulty and danger, and the end, inevitably, is tragic. Again the atmosphere of the Matter of Britain causes new literary ground to be broken. The central figures transcend both chivalric and amatory stereotypes. Tristan is versatile, a foreshadowing of the Renaissance man, not only a model knight but a musician, a linguist, a chess-player. Isolde is skilled in medical arts. Their story is the first major European instance of a mutual passion portrayed as a law unto itself, justifying almost any conduct that serves its ends, and, though sinful, excusable in the eyes of heaven.

The decline

Despite its splendour, King Arthur's golden age is doomed. Like all others it passes away. There is more here than nostalgia for a glory that no longer exists. There is grief for a glory actively destroyed.

For its destruction the Welsh supplied the first hint by telling of a battle of Camlann where Arthur fell. His opponents were not foreign enemies but other Britons; his own people were divided. Geoffrey interweaves Camlann with a motif of betrayal by a deputy-ruler, Arthur's nephew, whose variously spelt name is best known as Mordred. This is derived at several removes from 'Medraut', the name of someone said to have fallen in the same battle. The betrayal motif is not Welsh, and may have come from the actual betrayal of the British king, arguably Arthur's original, who was in Gaul in 468–70. Romancers take up the theme of a divided Round Table and carry it further, with implications that go beyond story-telling.

In the medieval Christian scheme, any golden-age myth, even one that was quasi-historical, could hardly fail to recall the Earthly Paradise of unfallen humanity. Dante makes that point in the *Divine Comedy*. Paradise, however, was Paradise Lost. Humanity transgressed, and fell. It followed that, while golden ages might be dreamed of or even realized, no society could regain the perfection which Adam forfeited, or sustain any special virtue it had. The loss, the fall, must be repeated. Individuals too, however noble, were liable to the same fate and very likely through their own shortcomings, since they shared in humanity's fundamental condition. They could not expect permanent success or felicity. A didactic image that recurs in the Middle Ages is that of Fortune's Wheel, which carries heroes and monarchs to the top, but dumps them on the downward side as it turns. That picture of the human lot is in the background of Arthurian literature as of any other. Although the Round Table affirms such lofty ideals, the seeds of disaster are planted early.

Even with Lancelot, who does largely live up to the ideals, his growing commitment to his love-affair is a cause of disruption and his very magnificence makes it one of the worst. The affair becomes a time-bomb that must explode sooner or later. Another theme which insinuates itself is that the traitor Mordred is a nemesis because he is really Arthur's son, begotten in incest with his half-sister Morgause. Arthur, it is said in extenuation, did not know who the lady was, but the sin remains a sin. These factors making for disaster are slow to come to a head. But human frailty of the same type begins causing trouble earlier, and so does another factor, magic.

Both combine to remove Merlin. Some accounts of his fate are kindlier than others. The essential story is that his departure was due to his obsessive desire for one of the Damsels of the Lake, sometimes called Nimue, sometimes Viviane. His own prophetic gift showed him that his pursuit of her would destroy him, yet he pursued. She was afraid of him, having heard that he was a devil's son, and she refused him as a lover. For her own ends she agreed to join him on a journey through Brittany and Cornwall, on the understanding that he would not use magic to subdue her physically. She learned many secrets from him. At length, having had enough, she used one of his own spells to shut him in an enchanted prison – a cave, or a tomb, or an enclosure with invisible walls. His final fate is doubtful.

Merlin's débâcle is a product, ironically, of the medieval idealization itself. The Celts, tolerant towards magic and pre-Christian things, would not have invented it; at any rate, not like this. But the golden age of Arthurian romance is evoked in the context of medieval, not Celtic Christianity, and this was harder, more black-and-white. Magic was believed in, but with less readiness to allow that it might be good, or even morally neutral. Helpful to Arthur as Merlin was made out to have been, and more than helpful, he was still given the diabolic paternity and said to have been preserved for his role only by his mother's virtue. With all his greatness, Christian romancers could not let him prosper too much. So, they decided, his sensual nature betrayed him, magic itself entrapped him, and Arthur lost him.

Tennyson's handling makes his downfall uglier. Vivien, as he calls the woman, is a mere seductress acting from hatred for the court. Merlin is old. The whole episode is unsavoury, and he lacks even the excuse of passion, not only because of his age but because he has no sexual interest in Vivien, and she has to work to arouse such interest as he is capable of. This symbolic destruction of wisdom is in keeping with the plan of the *Idylls*, which makes sensuality a major factor in undermining Arthurian ideals.

Something of the Celtic attitude may survive in Welsh legend, where Merlin's retirement is said to have been voluntary. He went to Bardsey Island off the north-western tip of Wales, and he is living on Bardsey still, perhaps asleep in an underground chamber, perhaps awake in an invisible house of glass, with nine companions. He has with him the Thirteen Treasures of Britain. These are talismans and relics concealed from the English. He also has the true British throne.

Yet even the Welsh acknowledge his separation from Arthur. The Christianity that dictated this affected another character, Morgan le Fay. In her origins Morgan is a Celtic goddess, or a blend of two goddess-figures: Matrona, a maternal river-deity, and the Irish Morrigan. She makes her literary début in Geoffrey's verse *Life of Merlin*, as a benign enchantress. French poets, inspired by Breton fairy-tales, introduce her in Arthur's infancy as a fairy godmother endowing him with good gifts. But under religious pressure the romancers turn her into another half-sister of the King, ambiguous, often malicious, a witch tutored by Merlin and a trouble-maker. Through Morgan too, magic becomes an influence that saps Camelot.

To revert to the time-bombs, Lancelot unwittingly plants another. The circumstances are strange, and so are the consequences when it at last

Merlin and Vivien, his temptress, as imagined by Tennyson. Seated under an oak, with chaplet, robe and long beard, the wizard is Druidic. The original sexual passion is absent and his response to Vivien, as shown by his relaxed hand, remains minimal. (Detail of illustration by Gustave Doré to Tennyson's Idylls of the King, *1868.)*

explodes. This is the reason for the Quest of the Grail. By a paradox the Quest too, though ostensibly holy, is on balance adverse to Camelot, because it lures away many knights on a time-consuming enterprise which few are fitted for, and from which a substantial number fail to return.

The Grail is a complex topic, and the accounts of it differ irreconcilably. Only the mainstream conceptions can be considered here. Its background is pre-Christian. There are Celtic legends of wonder-working vessels, horns of plenty, cauldrons of inspiration and regeneration. An early Welsh poem tells of Arthur and his companions going on a dangerous quest for a cauldron kept by nine maidens, in an Otherworld or Underworld known as Annwn. The word *graal* is Old French and means a large dish or serving-bowl. Chrétien de Troyes describes the youthful Perceval visiting a castle where the lord of the place is crippled by a wound. Perceval sees a maiden carrying a richly decorated graal, said to be a supernatural source of nourishment. He does not ask about this, and it transpires presently that he should have done so, and if he had, the lord would have been healed. Thus far we are in a realm of faerie. In the background are myths of vessels that are magical sources of life and well-being.

Soon afterwards a second poet, Robert de Boron, transforms the theme. In the hands of Robert and the romancers who follow him, the vessel becomes *the* Graal or Grail, the cup or dish used by Christ at the Last Supper to institute the sacrament. While the former associations are never quite lost, the focus shifts from physical to spiritual life. The Grail is said to have passed into the hands of Joseph of Arimathea, the rich man who obtained Christ's body after the crucifixion and provided the tomb. He caught drops of the sacred blood in it. As the 'Holy' Grail it had miraculous properties and gave its possessors a special link with God. A table was made to set it on, in memory of the table of the Last Supper. Relatives and friends of Joseph (the texts disagree as to whether he was with them himself) conveyed it to Britain, to the Vales of Avalon – that is, central Somerset, the future site of Glastonbury. Clearly the story is involved here with the legendary beginnings of Glastonbury Abbey, but the sources and interrelations are obscure. Then it passed into the custody of a series of Grail-keepers, collaterally descended from Joseph, who lived in a mysterious castle called Corbenic. The Grail, though enshrined out of sight, gave Britain a privileged place in Christendom, and was the medium of a special vision or revelation which could be attained by a worthy seeker.

That is the main picture, though it has many complications and variations. Early in Arthur's reign the current Grail-keeper, Pelles, decides that the time has come for a Grail-achiever to be born. He must be a perfect knight of the stock of Joseph, like Pelles himself. Achieving the Grail means more than simply locating it. Several knights discover the castle and witness apparitions and miracles, and, in some versions, undergo cryptic tests like Chrétien's hero. But none of the first generation look into the Grail and attain the ultimate vision, which seems to be a mystical knowledge of God, the Holy Trinity, the source through Christ of eternal life.

Pelles has a daughter, Elaine. When Lancelot happens to be at Corbenic, Pelles leads him to think that the Queen is in a castle near by. Elaine awaits him there, and Lancelot, bemused by a magic potion, goes to bed with her under the impression that she is Guinevere. Thus he begets a son, Galahad.

Galahad, the knight who eventually achieves the Grail, carrying the Grail Table with the aid of two companions. (Manuscript illustration, French, 14th c.)

Ironically, the amour that debars him from fully experiencing the Grail produces the perfect knight who can. Galahad, as an adult character, is meant to fuse religion with chivalry. If such a fusion were feasible, Arthur's golden age could be hallowed on a spiritual plane. But in its actual working-out through a specific figure, a chivalric saint, the conception fails. Galahad is handsome and courteous, a fighter equal to his father, but his total purity deprives him of human interest and sets him apart.

Lancelot's son is separated from him and brought up by nuns, away from court. Meanwhile conjectures gather around an empty chair at the Round Table, which, it will be remembered, was a deliberate echo of the Grail Table. The empty chair is called the Perilous Seat. This is the destined place of the Grail-achiever. When Galahad is in his late teens the nuns hand him over to Lancelot, not saying who he is, and asking only for sponsorship. The likeness is noticed and his identity realized. Lancelot himself keeps silence, and fights his son in a tournament like any other opponent. Though one would suppose that Galahad's education gave few facilities for training, he is a superlative knight, not only morally; he unhorses competitors till he and Lancelot are almost the sole survivors. Various signs, however, show that the Grail is to be his main concern, and he takes his place in the Perilous Seat.

When all the knights are assembled, a veiled apparition of the Grail circles through the hall above them. Many knights undertake the Quest: illogically perhaps, since Galahad is already marked out, but they hope at least to see more, and penetrate the mystery further. Arthur knows that the outcome will be sad, but he cannot stop them. A few come close and have glimpses, including Lancelot, ever noble in aspiration despite his sin. In the end the Grail passes from Britain to a distant country, Sarras. Galahad goes there, accompanied by Perceval and Bors, a cousin of Lancelot. In Sarras he attains the supreme vision . . . and dies. None of the rest have attained it. Some return, some do not. The end of the Quest is chiefly sorrow, and while relief is felt that it is over, Camelot is never the same again.

The passing of Arthur

The other time-bombs are still ticking. Mordred is nursing imagined grievances and planning to usurp the throne. Stability depends on the public unity of the royal couple. As to Guinevere's love-affair, Arthur is still either deceiving himself or turning a diplomatic blind eye. Agravain, a brother of Gawain, conspires with Mordred to force the issue into the open. Since infidelity by the Queen counts as treason, Arthur has to sentence her to be burnt at the stake. This is attempted at Carlisle, with a company of knights guarding the place of execution. Lancelot arrives with followers of his own, rescues Guinevere, and takes her to his castle Joyous Gard. In the course of the rescue he kills several knights, among them two more of Gawain's brothers, thus incurring Gawain's implacable enmity.

The Round Table is split between those faithful to the King and those sympathizing with Lancelot. Having restored Guinevere to her husband, Lancelot leads his supporters to his lands in France, where he sets up a rival kingdom. Arthur follows with an army, and tries to bring him under control, but Gawain's vendetta stands in the way of peace.

While Arthur is overseas his nemesis catches up with him. Geoffrey of Monmouth accounts for the foreign campaign differently, but the sequel is

Gawain's dead body, mourned by knights and by a lady who confesses that she loved him. Her infuriated husband strikes a blow at her with his sword. (Manuscript illustration, French, 14th c.)

much the same, and the developed story remains substantially his. Arthur has left Mordred in charge in Britain. Mordred treacherously proclaims that the King is dead, and has himself crowned. He enlists aid from the long-subdued Saxons, and even tries to marry Guinevere, but she eludes him and finds refuge in a convent. Arthur breaks off his continental campaign and returns home. Gawain dies from a wound at Dover, and reconciliation with Lancelot becomes possible, but there is no time to arrange it. Arthur leads his remaining loyalists to meet the traitor's army. The first clashes are promising but indecisive, and both leaders converge on a common doom.

The Camlann of the Welsh, where Arthur and 'Medraut' perish in an exterminatory conflict, cannot be pinned down convincingly. In medieval romance the battle shifts to Salisbury Plain, or, in Malory, 'a down beside Salisbury'. Malory makes it accidental. The King and Mordred meet to patch up a peace. Then a knight, stung in the foot by an adder, draws his sword to kill it, and his action is misconstrued and fighting breaks out. Most of the combatants are killed, including Mordred, and Arthur himself is badly wounded. The war is over, but so is his reign.

Romance adds some closing scenes. Most familiar is the image of the King commanding his last companion, Bedivere, to throw Excalibur into an expanse of water. The absence of any such expanse near Salisbury Plain is not felt as a problem. Bedivere is reluctant to sacrifice so splendid a weapon, so he hides it. Arthur sees through his evasions, and insists. When Bedivere does cast it away, an arm rises above the surface; the hand catches the sword and draws it under. The vanishing of Excalibur is one of several touches making it clear that Arthur's golden age is, so to speak, an emanation of himself. No successor can inherit his glory or prolong it.

A boat approaches bearing a group of ladies in mourning garb. Among them are Nimue and the ambiguous Morgan, now reconciled, and coming to convey the King to an enchanted place where his wound will be healed. This is the Isle of Avalon mentioned by Geoffrey as his last destination. Bedivere lowers him gently into the boat and it glides away out of sight. What then? Even before he was born, Merlin foretold that his departure would be shrouded in mystery, and so it is. Bedivere is shown what *may* be his grave, in a valley between two hills near Glastonbury. Nevertheless . . .

All this time Lancelot has been in France, with the knights who might have given Arthur the victory. News of events in Britain is slow to reach him. When it does he returns, but too late. He seeks out Guinevere in her convent and they take a sad farewell. Then he settles as a hermit in the valley near Glastonbury where – possibly – Bedivere saw Arthur's grave. Bedivere is already there, and other survivors join them, forming a small community. The crown of Britain, meanwhile, has passed to Constantine, a cousin of Arthur. But with the whole Round Table nobility dead, or abroad, or non-participating, continuity is broken for ever.

In Tennyson's treatment, the Queen's misconduct is not merely an occasion of the catastrophe but, in a long-term sense, the reason for it. Through most of the *Idylls* Mordred is a minor figure, a schemer but not a menace, till moral deterioration gives him his chance. Tennyson throughout is mindful of his allegory, of his story as 'shadowing Sense at war with Soul'. Therefore the royal amour becomes central. Sense is fighting back against

Soul at the very heart of the monarchy. The Queen and Lancelot set a fatal example that breeds cynicism about Christian matrimony, the sexual proprieties, and Arthur's ideals generally. With Merlin gone from much the same cause, and the Round Table weakened by the misguided Grail Quest, the slide towards ruin is inexorable.

Yet Tennyson's picture of the collapse is not wholly dominated by the one idea. He makes a more interesting addition. Right from the outset, doubts about Arthur's origin have been carefully planted. In the very first *Idyll* people are wondering who he is. A legitimate prince, Uther's son? or a child born out of wedlock and no true heir? or a being from the realm of faerie, swept in by the sea at Tintagel as an infant, and taken out of the water by Merlin? As long as he is successful, nobody cares, but towards the end, with his spell breaking, doubt revives as a serious issue and his right to rule is challenged. By making this final phase suggest genuine questions – Where does authority come from? Who has the right to demand such-and-such conduct, or impose such-and-such principles? And why? – Tennyson points to problems that subvert attempts to build real Utopias.

His account of Arthur's passing reinforces the symbolism. He brings the last battle back to Cornwall, or at least to Lyonesse. It is fought at the winter solstice, in a nightmare of gloom and mist where 'friend slew friend not knowing whom he slew', till the ideal kingdom has disintegrated and the knighthood is extinguished. Bedivere is left alone with the wounded King for the final scene.

Echoes of antiquity

To quote Malory:

> Some men say in many parts of England that King Arthur is not dead, but had by the will of Our Lord Jesu into another place; and men say that he shall come again.

It may seem unwise to approach a mysterious topic by way of a more mysterious topic. Yet it is worth looking at a pronouncement on Arthur by William Blake, whose Prophetic Books, with their extraordinary mythology, have stirred and puzzled generations of readers. In 1809 he exhibited some of his paintings, together with a Descriptive Catalogue. One of them, *The Ancient Britons*, is unhappily lost, but his long note on it survives. In this he wrote:

> The giant Albion, was Patriarch of the Atlantic; he is the Atlas of the Greeks, one of those the Greeks called Titans. The stories of Arthur are the acts of Albion, applied to a Prince of the fifth century.

Albion is an old name of Britain, and Blake's dictum might be taken to mean that the Arthurian legend is expressive of a nation which Albion, in a more perennial sense, personifies. But Albion here does more than personify. His role in Blake's abstruse and profound system, chiefly in the long poem *Jerusalem*, arises from theories current during the eighteenth century. In the same note the poet speaks of his country's ancient glory, 'when it was, as it again shall be, the source of learning and inspiration'. Enthusiasts such as Edward Davies, author of *Celtic Researches*, had argued that all the wisdom of antiquity – Greek, Indian, Persian, perhaps even (a daring suggestion) Hebrew – flowed from primordial British sages, proto-Druids. Blake took up the idea and generalized further: 'All things Begin & End in Albion's Ancient Druid Rocky Shore.' Therefore Albion, as universal culture-hero, could stand for the human race, both collectively and individually. In *Jerusalem* Albion's story is of humanity's fall into division and resurrection into unity. Because the primordial sages betrayed their trust, their golden age perished. The Albion of the poem, through his own errors, sinks into a deathlike sleep. The world as we know it in history, with its wars, lies, oppressions and corruptions, is the consequence: a kind of perverted creation. But at last he wakes – that is, Britain recovers her true nature and calling – and all is restored, transfigured in an apocalypse.

It is clear why Arthur is a reflection of Albion. Blake focuses on his deepest mythical quality. To quote the Descriptive Catalogue, legend tells of Arthur's 'death, or sleep, and promise to return again' The Arthur of legend, who presides over a golden age and passes away, is not dead. Like Albion in Blake's conception of history, he is gone, but will return; he is sleeping, but will awaken.

In the folklore account of his survival, which by-passes Avalon, he actually is sleeping. His hidden retreat is a cave. Sometimes he is said to have his knights with him, or his treasure, or both. One day he will emerge, to restore justice and peace throughout Britain. The cave legend is on record at Cadbury, the Somerset Camelot. It has several other locations. Normally the cave is concealed. It may open magically at long intervals, and a passer-by at that moment can see the sleeping King inside. Or a mysterious guide – Merlin himself, or the Scottish poet Thomas the Rhymer, who had connections with the realm of faerie – may conduct someone into it through a temporary gap or gate in a hillside. The visitor usually has cause for regret.

Where did this motif come from? Presumably it began somewhere, somehow. Europe has a number of similar tales, about Frederick Barbarossa and other heroes, but they do not seem to be very early, and may be echoes of the continental fame of Arthur himself. His own cave legend was soon known overseas. The only parallel case which looks plainly independent is that of the Mongolian Buddhist warrior Gesar, who, after an epic career, vanishes into a cave in the northern mountains. Yet Gesar does not seem to be sleeping. He lives in a secret paradisal place, Shambhala.

An inspiration for Arthur's cave legend was suggested almost a century ago and is probably the true one, because it accounts also for the other principal form of his immortality. Some say his wounds were healed in the Isle of Avalon and he is still there. His dual immortality looks as if it actually does derive from a British god resembling the chief Titan Cronus, whose myth was applied (as Blake puts it) to a prince of the fifth century.

This is one of the few myths of the British Celts recorded in pre-Christian times by an outside observer. He was a Roman official, Demetrius, who was in Britain in AD 82. His report is embedded in two works by Plutarch, written not long afterwards. The Britons who talked to him told him of an island far across the Atlantic, in the general direction of the summer sunset. They gave him (if Plutarch is to be trusted) a good deal of geographical detail. The island, they said, was beautiful, with a gentle climate, and in it was a deep cavern where an exiled god lay asleep, on rock that looked like gold. Around him were spirits who had been his attendants when he was powerful in the world. He had prophetic dreams which they interpreted. He was there because a junior god had supplanted him. The supplanter allowed him this honourable banishment, with sleep in place of physical bonds.

That at least is what the Britons are reported as saying. Unfortunately Plutarch does what classical authors are apt to do when dealing with foreign gods and myths. Instead of giving the real names and details, he resorts to parallels, assuming here that the British myth is the same the Greeks told of Cronus, banished by his son Zeus to a western Elysium. In consequence, the god is presented as the chief Titan in person, with embellishments that are purely Greek and added by Plutarch for literary purposes. Still, there is no reason to question the essential story or its British provenance. This is surely the ultimate source of both main versions of Arthur's survival: a departed golden-age god on a western island, sleeping in a cave with companions around him. That myth drifted down from pagan Britons to Arthurian story-tellers, and some opted for the island, some for the cave.

Avalon

While folklore prefers the cave as Arthur's retreat, literary imagination prefers the island, and a waking rather than a slumbering Arthur. Geoffrey mentions Avalon twice in his *History*, saying that Arthur's sword was forged there, and later introducing it in its more famous capacity, as the island where he was taken after his last battle 'so that his wounds might be attended to'. 'Avalon', which corresponds to a Welsh *Avallach*, is usually thought to be derived from a word for 'apple'. Geoffrey takes it in that sense when he reverts to the subject in his verse *Life of Merlin*, where the bard Taliesin relates how he and several companions conveyed the wounded King to the apple-island. This is the passage where Morgan makes her pleasant début, ruling the island as head of a sisterhood of nine. She has Arthur placed on a golden bed, examines the damage, and undertakes to heal him if he will stay there long enough.

Morgan, as remarked, is here a goddess-figure, domesticated by the Celts' easy-going Christianity. Her community recalls an actual group of nine priestesses, who, in Roman times, lived on an island off the coast of Brittany. It also recalls the nine maidens in the Welsh Otherworld, who watch over the cauldron which Arthur seeks in a foreshadowing of the Grail Quest.

Layamon, the author of an English narrative poem based on Geoffrey, is the first to describe women as bearing Arthur away over the water, not simply receiving him on arrival. Morgan (he calls her Argante, but manifestly has the same lady in mind) is 'a fay most fair' dwelling in Avalon. Malory improves the story of the departure. While he testifies to belief in the return, he is cautious about it.

There are no good grounds for the theory that Avalon was a Celtic abode of the dead. Its Otherworld quality has more the nature of fairyland, and whatever departed spirits it may have harboured, the point of Arthur's own sojourn is, precisely, that he is not dead. Few of the romancers have anything to add on the topic, and those who have treat it fancifully, even putting Avalon in the Mediterranean. A notion that it was Sicily explains why a mirage phenomenon in the Straits of Messina is named after the enchantress, Fata Morgana.

Geoffrey gives no warrant for such fantasies, and he is still in touch with authentic mythology. He tries to give Avalon credibility by listing it with a number of other islands, some real, some drawn from literature. He calls it a Fortunate Isle, taking the epithet from classical legend. The Fortunate Isles were sometimes identified with the western Elysium, where Cronus lived and his golden age was still going on. Heroes beloved of the gods dwelt there in happiness without death. Geoffrey's similar Avalon is over vague western waters. Besides its classical antecedents, it has links with the Celts not only in Wales but in Ireland. We are dealing with a common stock of mythology, some of it very ancient.

The Irish had far-ranging ideas about a paradisal west. It contained an apple-isle of their own, Emain Ablach, the favoured dwelling of the sea-god Manannan. Emain Ablach was only one island in an Atlantic archipelago, stretching into the sunset with no known limit. Tir na nOg was there, the Land of the Young, and so was a Land of Women, fairy-folk resembling Morgan's sisterhood. Irish romances tell of voyagers – Bran, Mael Duin, and others – who visited some of the islands and had extraordinary adventures. Most famous of these romances is a Christian one, the *Voyage of St Brendan*. In the Middle Ages the tale of Brendan spread beyond Celtic lands like the tales of Arthur, and was sometimes regarded as an offshoot of the Matter of Britain.

The Chinese too had an island of immortality. Its name was P'eng-lai, and it was out in the Pacific, not very far off. It figures in the lore of Taoist alchemy. The alchemists, who sought the Elixir of Life, believed that P'eng-lai was the home of immortal sages possessing the secret.

Avalon has a second meaning which seems to contradict the first. In the outcome, however, it may not be so different. Not all the Welsh asserted Arthur's survival. According to a bardic verse, his grave was a mystery. This might mean that his whole demise was a mystery, so that he could indeed be alive. But it might be understood in a narrower sense – that he was dead, but his place of burial was unknown, or a well-kept secret. The second interpretation made its mark late in the twelfth century. Reputedly a bard told Henry II that Arthur was dead indeed, and his remains lay in the graveyard of Glastonbury Abbey, between two memorial pillars, at a great depth.

In 1190 or early '91, after an excavation, the Abbey announced that the clue had been followed up and the grave discovered. The diggers had struck a stone slab embedded in the ground, and underneath it a lead cross with a Latin inscription meaning 'Here lies buried the renowned King Arthur in the Isle of Avalon.' Farther down they unearthed a coffin made of a hollowed-out log. Inside were the bones of a tall man, who had evidently received a blow on the head, because the skull was damaged. With these were the smaller bones of a woman, taken to be Guinevere. The relics were enshrined in the Abbey church. It must be pointed out that two romances which mention Arthur's supposed burial imply that he was laid to rest, if he was, in a Christian community on higher ground, so that his bones must have been transferred to the Abbey site when the community moved downhill itself. But the early location is seriously possible, quite apart from the question of the grave, so no problem need arise.

Glastonbury, or rather the hill-cluster in which it is cradled, and which *was* once almost insular, was now accepted by many as the true Avalon, Arthur's last destination. Robert de Boron, the first to relate the Grail's early history, told soon afterwards of the Grail being brought to the 'Vales' of Avalon, meaning central Somerset where the Abbey subsequently stood. It was helpful that all this area was apple-growing country, as it still is. Morgan was retained in the story as a lady who owned the Isle and tried unsuccessfully to heal Arthur's wounds.

Some historians have argued that the grave was a fake, a publicity stunt on the monks' part, their presumed object being to raise funds for rebuilding after a fire. However, there is no evidence that they did exploit the grave to raise funds. It went unchallenged by the Welsh – one or two Welsh authors drew particular attention to it – and no rival burial site was ever produced, even by persons who had a motive to discredit Glastonbury. It is likely that there was at least a Welsh tradition of Arthur's burial there, which could not be denied once the bard had divulged it and the monks, seemingly, had verified it.

Modern excavation has proved that they dug where they said and found an early burial, with signs that whoever was interred was of some importance. The only question is who it was, and the answer depends on whether the cross with Arthur's name on it was genuine or a forgery. While the cross has disappeared, a picture of it survives – and is inconclusive. On the one hand, the word 'renowned', *inclitus*, is used by Geoffrey in telling of Arthur's passing, so that the inscription on the cross might have been concocted by someone with Geoffrey's book in front of him. On the other hand, the style and irregularity of the lettering, and an archaic peculiarity in the spelling, tell against a twelfth-century forgery.

Whether or not the hill-cluster was called Avalon in earlier times, it certainly had an otherworldly aura that made the identification apt and credible. A Celtic name for it, Ynys-witrin, the Isle of Glass, favoured the general atmosphere of faerie. This in turn may have had something to do with its Grail connection, and the claim that the first church on the site (the first in Britain, said the monks) was built by Joseph of Arimathea, the Grail-bearer.

Behind the Glastonbury mythology – of which there is much more, some of it ancient, some medieval, some modern – is probably the fact that the place was a pagan sanctuary before it was Christian. One reason for thinking so is the dedication of the first church, the Old Church as it was called. There is no authentic record of its foundation; hence the legends of Joseph and so forth. But it seems to have been in existence during the first half of the sixth century. The dedication was to the Virgin Mary, a celestial patronage rare at that date in western Europe, and unparalleled in Britain. The Old Church may have been a unique British product of the first wave of Marian devotion, in Late Roman times. In that phase the Virgin sometimes took the place of a long-established goddess, as at Ephesus, the city of Artemis ('Diana of the Ephesians'), where the cult of the Mother of God was sanctioned by a Church council in 431. Our Lady of Glastonbury may have had a similar background.

However, pre-Christian interest focuses mainly on the Tor, the highest hill in the cluster, well known for its ruined tower on top. This is the remnant of another church, a medieval one, dedicated to St Michael. The motive may have been his role as conqueror of the infernal powers. According to immemorial belief, the Tor is hollow, an entrance to Annwn, the

The Cretan Labyrinth, with Theseus killing the Minotaur: a medieval portrayal. It resembles Greek and Roman representations, but is more complex, with a larger number of circuits. (Manuscript illustration, 12th c.)

Otherworld where Arthur went in quest of the cauldron with its maiden guardians. Legend tells of St Collen, a wandering Welsh holy man, going inside the Tor and trying to exorcize Annwn's ruler, Gwyn, with his court of fairy-folk.

A clue to such ideas may lie in the earthwork terraces surrounding the hill. The notion that they are agricultural strip-lynchets is not tenable. A theory with reputable, if cautious, archaeological support is that they are remains of a prehistoric ritual track, winding around seven times, in a back-and-forth maze pattern that occurs very widely. On Cretan coins it is a representation of the famous Labyrinth.

A Cretan text refers to a goddess as 'Mistress' of the Labyrinth. Ariadne, who guides Theseus, is doubtless a form of her. Occurrences of the theme in other places suggest that this myth was sometimes given a more masculine bias, turning the goddess into an imprisoned woman whom a hero had to extricate by threading the maze. In the Indian epic *Ramayana*, Rama's wife Sita is immured by an abductor in his fortress in Lanka, and an eleventh-century illustration shows her inside a maze on the same pattern. To return to Britain, in the oldest known version of a recurrent tale of the kidnapping of Guinevere, her kidnapper takes her to Glastonbury and Arthur has to go there to get her back; and excavation has revealed traces of what may have been a fort on top of the Tor, at the heart of the hypothetical maze, and dating from the Arthurian period.

Glastonbury's mythos, both Christian and (apparently) pre-Christian, ensured that Arthur's grave could not make an end of him. He was absorbed into an Avalonian mystique which itself came to include a survival-and-resurrection motif. The Abbey was dissolved in 1539 and fell gradually into ruin. But Austin Ringwode, the last of the monks (more probably a layman in the service of the community), is said to have foretold on his deathbed that, after the desolation, Glastonbury would rise again, and then 'peace and plenty would for a long time abound'. The rediscovery of his prophecy, whether authentic or spurious, has played a part in a real resurgence: not only of Christian Glastonbury but of the place's inferred senior status as a mystical power-centre, an 'alternative' spiritual capital. While modern Glastonbury has been dubbed the 'last bastion of hippy culture', the 'Mecca of New Age lifestyle', there is more to this than media comedy. One of several manifestations, taking serious artistic and dramatic forms, has been an attempt to reinstate the original Goddess.

The return of the king

The germ of the belief in Arthur's continuance was a phenomenon found in other contexts. What is special is not that it was held, but that it acquired the mythic dimensions it did. While the starting-point cannot be documented, it was doubtless no more than the recurrent reluctance to accept someone's extinction, someone regarded as important. This is not merely outmoded superstition. James Joyce notes a report among Irish patriots that Charles Stuart Parnell, far from being hounded to death by his enemies, escaped to South Africa. During the First World War, British public opinion rejected the loss at sea of Lord Kitchener, architect of the war-effort, and invented an undercover mission in Russia. The subjects of such rumours need not be 'good'. Similar tales were told of Nero and Hitler. Usually, however, the survivor is somebody whom many would wish to believe in.

A recent case-history, outstanding because of its adaptation of Arthur himself, is that of John F. Kennedy. His conversion into an American Arthur was retrospective. In his short presidency he acquired an aura of youth, glamour and hope, but with no specific Arthurian hints, beyond his enjoyment of the musical *Camelot*. Myth-making began on the day of his assassination in Dallas. The historian Theodore H. White (another T.H. White: odd coincidence) soon took up the *Camelot* hint in *Life* magazine, quoting the line from the musical's closing scene about 'one brief shining moment'. Kennedy's survival legend made him a new Arthur more precisely. Persisting into the seventies, it claimed that the supposedly fatal bullet had failed to kill him. It had, however, caused incapacitating brain damage. Doctors were keeping him on a life-support machine and cherishing hopes that he might, like Arthur, be healed of his wound. The story gradually faded out, and Kennedy's glamour faded too, though never completely. In the late eighties Americans discovered a new survivor, Elvis Presley, who was sighted prosaically in supermarkets.

Arthur was more than any of these. He went beyond simple survival. To begin with, he became immortal where they did not. A Parnell, a Kitchener, a Hitler might not have died when alleged, but would presumably be dead by now. There were others, though, with whom the presumption was not admitted, and one of them may offer a clue as to how an original Arthur could have broken the barrier. This is the Portuguese king Sebastian, who led an expedition against the Moors in 1578. He was routed and reported dead, after which the Spanish annexed Portugal. Understandably it soon began to be whispered that no one had seen him fall. He was still alive, and would come back to liberate his country. The hope persisted despite the discrediting of four pretenders. More remarkably, though Portugal regained independence in 1640, Sebastian was not consigned to oblivion. In 1807 he was looked for as a leader against Napoleon. Even today, aboriginal tribes in the former Portuguese colony of Brazil dream of Sebastian as a demigod who will cross the ocean to save them from oppression and poverty.

Here we plainly come closer to Arthur. Perhaps his own death was traditionally doubtful. Anyhow, in his immortality, he was at first like Sebastian: an undying Celtic Messiah who would restore the fortunes of the Britons' descendants in Wales, Cornwall and Brittany. Very possibly it was thanks to his literary fame that the cave legend became attached in the Middle Ages to other heroes, even without a Sebastian-type basis in factual doubt, or a Sebastian-type expectation. The best-known instance is the German emperor Frederick – originally Frederick II, later Frederick I, Barbarossa – who sleeps in the Kyffhäuser mountain. According to the folklorist Jennifer Westwood, most of these sleeping heroes are historical. However mythic its remote inspiration, the motif seldom or never gets applied to fairy-tale characters. So Arthur's cave legend tells in favour of his reality, in some sense.

One or two of the European sleepers are vaguely imagined returning some day, like Sebastian and Arthur himself. Yet Arthur's return is greater than theirs. Again he takes a step beyond. Because of his golden-age aura, his return implies a real difference in the world. His adoption by the English and others makes him more than a champion of the Celtic fringe. He will reappear, says prophecy, in the hour of Britain's need; and his reappearance, if imagined at all, can hardly be restricted to military action. At the very least he will bring another brief shining moment.

Blake's insight is sound when he makes Arthur reflect his symbolic Albion, whose sleep is a decline into strife and darkness, and whose waking is an apocalyptic rebirth. This is no abstract fancy. Arthur's golden-age myth expresses a mode of thought and action, a syndrome or archetype, that actually happens. While the phrase 'golden age' can be applied loosely to any good, creative or prosperous period, history attests a persistent compulsion to resurrect its older, more exact sense: to believe in a *lost* golden age, long ago, with a unique significance. This takes on a variety of guises. As remarked, a main reason for Arthur's fascination is the way his legend gives shape and substance to a perennial dream. In China, the early Chou period; in India, the Krita Yuga; in Greece, the era of Cronus and the Titans: all embody much the same notion. But this is more than an ancient mythical theme. It is an attitude, a way-of-looking-at-things, which can have potent effects. Again and again, 'the golden age' is an apt term for something seriously believed in, a long-lost glory or promise; and again and again, Arthur's return is an eloquent metaphor for something further believed – that the long-lost glory or promise is not truly lost, and can be reinstated for a fresh start, with intervening corruption swept away.

Arthur himself was exploited thus by Henry Tudor, who became Henry VII in 1485 by overthrowing Richard III, and restored relative peace after the Wars of the Roses. He was partly Welsh, with a pedigree going back to reputed relatives of Arthur. Propagandists proclaimed that Henry was restoring the true British monarchy after the long break. He gave the name Arthur to his firstborn son, intending that he should reign as Arthur II, and complete the prophecy's fulfilment. The plan failed because Prince Arthur died young. Nevertheless this Tudor myth survived to be elaborated by Spenser in *The Faerie Queene*.

More interesting, however, are the ideas of activists who had no thought of Arthur, would not have dreamed of invoking his legend, and, in some cases, may never have heard of him.

In the sixteenth century, Christian reformers were agreed that the Church was corrupt, though Catholics and Protestants disagreed as to the remedy. But neither party talked of development or liberalization in the style of many Christians today. Both appealed to the Church's golden age of purity, the time of the Apostles and maybe a hundred years or so after, and called for its recovery.

In the eighteenth century, Rousseau supplied a mystique for the French Revolution. The conception of progress was in the air, but his doctrines were not progressive. They asserted a primitive, unspoilt human nature, and a good, free, equal society living the simple life long ago. This had been subverted by the selfish abuse of individual talent, by the accumulation of wealth, by civilization as it has been up to now, and by various resulting blights such as kings and priests. The proper course was to restore it, as far as feasible, by totally changing institutions and getting rid of the blights. This was to be accomplished, not by reform, but by a titanic upsurge of a mystically conceived 'general will', the deep instinctive wisdom of a society, even a misled and corrupted society. For Rousseau's disciples the Revolution was not an evolution, it was an apocalyptic fresh start.

In the nineteenth century, Marx and Engels worked out their system on the basis of an interpretation of history. They announced it in the *Communist Manifesto*. Originally there was no golden age at the beginning. Society was portrayed as simply evolving through a series of class oligarchies and class conflicts. Later, however, Marx read a study of the Iroquois by the anthropologist Lewis H. Morgan, and concluded that a 'primitive communism', quite like Rousseau's natural society, did once exist. Engels expanded Marx's notes into a book of his own, and tacked on 'primitive communism' at the beginning of the historical process. Thus even Marxism, which purported to be scientific, yielded to the need for a golden age. Lenin developed the idea, arguing that after the revolution oppressive power-structures would wither away, if perhaps not very soon, and the lost classless idyll would be reborn on a higher level.

In the twentieth century, Afro-Asian nationalism began with the uprising of India under British rule. Westernized Indians called for an India that would be industrial, parliamentary, progressive. They completely failed to rouse the masses. The leader who did rouse them was Mahatma Gandhi, who rejected all such things as corruptions, appealed to a submerged India of saints and sages and village communes and handicrafts, and tried – through his spinning-wheel programme, for instance – to bring at least some of it back. His success was in large-scale inspiration rather than large-scale results, but the inspiration was powerful enough to make political action effective.

A further, recent instance is the growth of golden-age thinking in the women's movement. Drawing on the poetic intuitions of Robert Graves, and the archaeological theories of Marija Gimbutas, feminists have aired the notion of an ancient 'matristic' society, worshipping The Goddess rather than gods, when the sexes were in a correct balance and women had their proper status. It was destroyed, they claim, by conquerors who created a 'patriarchal' society, ruled by men and sustained by the supremacy of male deities. Balance and justice can be restored through an informed women's movement and the Goddess's reinstatement.

These are simply conspicuous cases, and examples could be multiplied. Even the cool Confucius was thinking on the same lines when he spoke of reviving the Way of the Former Kings, and so was Virgil when he saluted Augustus as restorer of the *Saturnia regna*. Why such a persistent, often irrational, compulsion? A psychologist might see nothing in it but a kind of nostalgia, a projection of rose-tinted childhood and the longing to recapture youth. Arthur himself, as a symbol of this way-of-looking-at-things, might be forced into such a mould. But while no other mythology has an Arthur exactly, several have gods and superhuman beings who are like enough to require that the explanation should fit them, yet do not seem amenable to it.

Take, for instance, the Mexican god Quetzalcoatl, the Feathered Serpent. He had a human form. In that form, according to the Aztecs, he crossed the Gulf of Mexico and arrived on the mainland early in the Christian era. He reigned at Tula, north of the present Mexico City, as king, priest and prophet, and taught the surrounding tribes to farm the land and work metals, to build houses and keep a calendar. A rival god, Tezcatlipoca, drove him out. He went to Cholula, then to the coast in the Tabasco area, and departed over the sea on a raft . . . or maybe the waves parted to let him through. At

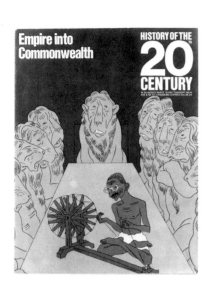

Gandhi at his spinning-wheel, defying British imperial power with an ancient and holy simplicity that proved hard to handle. (German cartoon, originally published in Simplicissimus, *1931.)*

30

any rate, he made it clear that he would return. When the Spanish landed, in 1519, the Aztec emperor Montezuma suspected that their leader Cortes *was* Quetzalcoatl and should be appeased rather than resisted. The conquest was thereby made much easier. Another version of the legend was current in Peru, where the god was called Viracocha.

Hinduism's golden age, the Krita Yuga, has passed away like the rest. But when the present aeon is collapsing, Vishnu will take shape as the Messiah Kalki, abolishing the degenerate world, and ushering in a new Krita Yuga. His manifestation is to begin at a place called Sambhala or Shambhala. In Hindu teaching this has seldom been stressed, but it became part of the lore of an Indian school of Buddhism that was carried into Tibet and Mongolia. The name was applied to an abode of wisdom and spiritual power in a paradisal valley among the northern mountains The Messianic motif was transplanted. This is where we make contact with the Mongolian Buddhist hero who resembles Arthur. After glorious exploits Gesar vanishes from the world, but he is destined to re-emerge from Shambhala as a champion of the Mongol people. The secret paradise of Shambhala probably supplied a hint for James Hilton's Shangri-la.

We are dealing with a cluster of themes, which have strong enough affinities to produce overlaps and blendings, but cannot be reduced simplistically to guises of a single myth, about childhood or anything else. Arthur is the figure in whom they converge most powerfully. To focus on the golden age as known in the west, and the syndrome corresponding to it, there is much to be said for Dante's suggestion: that behind such legends and fancies is the tradition of a lost Eden of unfallen humanity. *Genesis*-type mythology as a source is arguable, and perhaps relevant in Asia too. The substratum of the syndrome would be, in essence, Paradise-Lost-and-Regained, whether this comes from Christianity, or from a lingering Christian afterglow, or from some other element in myth or prehistory to which Christian doctrine gave a particular form. In Christian terms, the legend-weavers and ideologues are expressing a sense of Fall and Redemption, of departed beatitude and encroaching death and possible deliverance, that is integral to the human condition.

That is one reason why Arthur with his second coming is not an echo of Christ with his. Christ at his first coming is not, like Arthur, a golden-age figure. He has no political power and only local fame. Rejection of earthly greatness is part of his mission, as the Temptation story shows. In the milieu of the Bible, Arthur's dual manifestation corresponds rather to the first chapters and the last.

The Christian golden age is, as Dante indicates, the happy state of Adam and Eve in the Garden of Eden. The tree of life grows in it (*Genesis* 2:9) and they are free to eat its fruit and live for ever. But a malignant being undermines them and destroys their blessedness. Their fall, through eating the fruit of the other, forbidden, tree, brings death into the world, because they are expelled from Eden and debarred from the tree of life (3:22–4). At the end of the Bible in *Revelation*, chapters 21–2, the New Jerusalem, however interpreted, is Paradise Regained. The restoration is underlined by the fact that the tree of life grows there, as foreshadowed near the beginning of the book (2:7) and now explicitly stated near the end (22:2, 14, 19). The redeemed have free access to it as Adam and Eve had before their fall.

Whatever the nature of the ultimate sources, Arthur symbolizes a deeply rooted factor in human nature. Much of his spell is due to his standing for a golden age, a potent theme in any case. But because of his immortality, the golden age, though eclipsed, has the implicit quality of being still potentially 'there', as so many have desired their golden ages to be; and his predicted return expresses its power to reawaken. Few today would believe literally in Arthur's survival, or, indeed, in this particular golden age. He still strikes a chord to which literal belief is irrelevant, and which reverberates far outside his own legend.

King Arthur is depicted as one of the Nine Worthies, a group of heroes familiar in medieval art and literature. 'Worthy' here implies greatness and martial prowess. The nine are first listed in 1310 or thereabouts by Jacques de Longuyon. Three are Jewish – Joshua, David and Judas Maccabaeus; three pagan – Hector, Alexander and Caesar; and three Christian – Arthur, Charlemagne and Godfrey of Bouillon. Jacques gives an account of Arthur derived from Geoffrey of Monmouth's *History of the Kings of Britain*, to show that the Briton ranks with the other eight as a noble ruler and mighty warrior. (Detail from a French tapestry, c. 1385.)

Arthur's magical proof of kingship is known as the 'Sword in the Stone' test, though it varies slightly. A stone block has a sword stuck in it, which only the rightful king can pull out. Sometimes, as here, the sword is in an anvil on top of the stone. The test's precise meaning alters. At first, Arthur's ability to draw the sword is a sign of God's approval. In better-known versions, the test proves his royal identity against challengers. (Flemish manuscript illustration, c. 1290.)

Riding before Camelot with a company of knights (right), the King shows his uniqueness. Camelot is not Britain's capital, it is the chief residence of Arthur alone, focal to his golden age. According to some stories, after he passed away the vindictive Mark of Cornwall marched to Camelot and destroyed it. This conception of a personal headquarters may owe something to traditions about the hill-fort Cadbury Castle, the Somerset 'Camelot'. (French manuscript illustration, late 15th c.)

Arthur's army confronting the Saxons: from a fifteenth-century chronicle of Hainaut in Belgium. The chronicler, Jean Wauquelin, made a French translation of Geoffrey's *History* and drew on it in the chronicle to give an account of Arthur, in the belief that Hainaut was part of his empire. In the picture, by Guillaume Vrelant, Arthur is fighting the real enemies of the Post-Roman Britons, and to that extent the chronicle is in touch with history. But the practice of updating has turned both armies into medieval forces, with a background of medieval buildings. The bishop beside Arthur is Dubricius – St Dyfrig, a real person, promoted by Geoffrey to national importance. He is still important in Tennyson's *Idylls*, where he officiates at the wedding of Arthur and Guinevere. (Flemish manuscript illustration, *c.* 1468.)

The child with a special destiny . . . Merlin has dealings with Tristan's parents as well as Arthur's. King Meliodas of Lyonesse marries Elizabeth, sister of King Mark of Cornwall. She dies giving birth to Tristan while Meliodas is imprisoned under a spell. Merlin brings about his release. After seven years he remarries. Tristan, whose life is endangered by his stepmother, has to be removed from the parental home. On Merlin's advice, Meliodas entrusts him to a tutor, Governal (below), who takes him to France for his education. (French manuscript illustration early 15th c.) Other mythologies tell of similar cases. The young Achilles is brought up by the wise centaur Cheiron. In an eastern variation (left) the future Buddha is under the protection of Lao-tsu and Confucius, founder-figures of China's senior religions, which were helpful rather than adverse to Buddhism taking a Chinese form. (Chinese painting on silk, 14th c.)

Michael the archangel (left) is the celestial lord of Mont-Saint-Michel in Normandy, the abode of a cannibal giant slain by Arthur. He is chief of the heavenly host, vanquisher of the satanic powers. His name is Hebrew and means 'Who is like God?' Michael appears on the Arthurian scene at Glastonbury, where the church on the Tor was dedicated to him. (Italian manuscript illustration, c. 1490.)

The giant whom Arthur fights on Mont-Saint-Michel (above) has come from Spain and taken possession. Arthur's cleansing of the Mount may echo some legend of the archangel himself, since this giant is diabolically evil. Giant-killing is part of the general extirpation of monsters that is expected of heroes. Arthur has two principal gigantic opponents. The other, living on Snowdon, makes himself a cloak from the beards of slain kings and tries to add Arthur's to it. (English manuscript illustration, 15th c.)

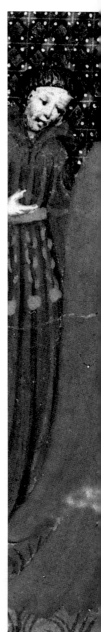

Christ and his apostles (left) seated at the Last Supper. Arthurian romancers assume that the table was round, thus making Arthur's Round Table a link between his regime and the foundation of Christianity. The cup in front of Jesus acquires mystical attributes as the Holy Grail. (French manuscript illustration, 15th c.)

Below is a version of the Round Table of Arthur. When this is mentioned first, its stated purpose is to prevent quarrels over precedence. In romance it becomes an object of deeper significance, made by Merlin, and symbolizing the round world and heavens. It also commemorates the table on which Joseph of Arimathea

kept the Grail, which, in turn, commemorated the table of the Last Supper. A place called the Perilous Seat corresponds to the place of Judas. No Round Table could really have accommodated all the knights, and some artists assume that only a few sat down at a time. (French manuscript illustration, 15th c.)

le siege arla

Chivalry and sex: an Italian scene of *The Triumph of Venus* (left) depicts six famous characters adoring the love-goddess. The Arthurian figures are Tristan (wearing a peaked hat) and Lancelot. With them are heroes of Trojan legend, and Samson. Both Arthurian knights are devoted to married women, in a kind of relationship approved by the Courtly Love code. But with both, the relationship goes beyond. Arthurian romance breaks new ground in amatory literature. (Painted tray by the Master of Taranto, early 15th c.)

Chivalry and chastity: Galahad occupies the Perilous Seat (below), the destined place of the knight who will achieve the Quest of the Grail. He is Lancelot's son, begotten through a magical trick. While Lancelot's adulterous passion prevents him from attaining the ultimate Grail vision, it produces a faultless offspring who can. Pre-eminent in manly deeds, but totally chaste, Galahad combines chivalry with spirituality. Yet his origin leaves a reader wondering about the author – quite possibly a cleric – who invented it. (French manuscript illustration, 15th c.)

Merlin makes his début in Geoffrey's *History*, confronting the usurper Vortigern, showing him two fighting dragons (below), and revealing how they portend Britain's future. Afterwards he becomes an adviser to the two legitimate kings preceding Arthur, Aurelius Ambrosius and Uther. Curiously, Geoffrey does not bring Merlin to the court of Arthur himself, but romancers make him the key figure in establishing Arthur's kingship. (English manuscript illustration, 15th c.)

In T.H. White's novels his role is developed still further. He is seen here (right) as played by Laurence Naismith in the film musical *Camelot* (1967) based on White. The owl's name is Archimedes.

Krishna in the Hindu epic *Mahabharata* (left) is perhaps the best parallel to Merlin from another mythology. An avatar or incarnation of the god Vishnu, he aids the righteous king Yudhishthir and his brothers against their unscrupulous cousin Duryodhana. His special friend among the brothers is Arjuna, to whom, as here, he gives spiritual instruction. (Indian miniature, Rajasthan, 1753.)

Sacred and profane love. Both become adverse to the Arthurian fellowship. When Galahad is marked out as Grail-achiever, numerous other knights (including Lancelot, below) desert their posts to go on the Quest. But the love of God, in the form of a full religious vocation, is not for them. Their salvation lies in rightly living the lives they are fitted for. Many never return, and their replacements are of inferior quality. (French manuscript illustration, 15th c.)

Lancelot and Guinevere take their first kiss at a meeting contrived by Galleot as go-between (right). Dante recalls this fatal encounter when he tells the story of Paolo and Francesca, who read about it together and become lovers. A 'courtly' relationship, simply as adoration of another man's wife, need not go further. With Lancelot and Guinevere it does go further, ending in catastrophe when Arthur has to punish the Queen, and the knights take sides. (French manuscript illustration, c. 1405.)

A recurrent triad of Celtic goddess-figures, which, in Britain, represented one goddess manifested in three forms. Perhaps a mythic antecedent for Guinevere, or Gwenhwyfar as she is called in Wales. A summary of bardic tradition refers cryptically to 'Arthur's Three Great Queens', all named Gwenhwyfar. Even in medieval texts the Queen has a kind of doppelganger who causes confusion. The notion of her as somehow multiple may go back to Celtic queenship embodying the divinity of the Triple Goddess. (Romano-Celtic stone relief, France.)

Guinevere at the other extreme, reduced to humanity and frailty. As a Celtic queen, with or without a divine aspect, she would have been her husband's equal. When she is adopted by medieval writers with different standards, her equality comes through as self-will, her freedom to take lovers comes through as infidelity. Later again, her love for Lancelot makes her wicked to some authors, tragic to others. (Photograph by Julia Margaret Cameron, 1874.)

George Clifford, Earl of Cumberland, at a tournament in 1590 on the anniversary of Elizabeth I's accession. As Queen's Champion, he styled himself Knight of Pendragon Castle. This castle, in his Cumbrian earldom, allegedly stood on the site of an older one belonging to Arthur's father Uther, called the Pendragon (Foremost Leader). Tudor propagandists claimed that the dynasty's part-Welsh founder, Henry VII, had restored the true 'British' monarchy, and in 1590 Spenser had just published the first books of *The Faerie Queene*, flattering Elizabeth in the light of this myth. (Miniature by Nicholas Hilliard, *c.* 1590.)

A knight at the Eglinton Tournament, held in 1839 (right). In the eighteenth century the Arthurian legend had been neglected, but now, thanks largely to Sir Walter Scott, romantic medievalism was gaining ground and beginning to inspire new treatments of it. The Tournament, at Eglinton Castle in Ayrshire, was conceived in the same spirit. Rain unfortunately restricted the programme. (Painting by Henry Corbould, *c.* 1839.)

Geoffrey makes the revolt of Mordred, Arthur's nephew and trusted deputy, the immediate cause of his downfall. Older Welsh matter mentions 'Medraut' but no betrayal. Geoffrey seems to be drawing on a non-Welsh source.

The Christian archetype of treachery is Judas's betrayal of Jesus. Dante puts traitors at the bottom of hell, with Judas the prey of Satan himself. Arthur's overthrow is atrociously wicked. But some authors make it a kind of retribution, Mordred being his incestuously begotten son. (Painted predella by Ugolino di Nerio, Italy, early 14th c.)

54

Arthur and Mordred meet in a battle which is fatal to both, and to most of the participants. Reputedly fought at a place called Camlann, it has been claimed as the best-attested Arthurian event. However, attempts to relate various proposed Camlanns to the actual story have yielded no firm conclusion. Leading romancers drop the name 'Camlann' and locate the battle near Salisbury. (English manuscript illustration, 15th c.)

Arthur's army fighting Mordred's. The picture is double. On the left the battle is raging, with both leaders active. On the right the wounded King has been laid in a wagon. The devices on the shields show medieval attempts at Arthurian heraldry. A fifteenth-century 'roll of arms' ascribed to Jacques d'Armagnac gives a list of the knights' supposed emblems. (Flemish manuscript illustration, early 14th c.)

Excalibur departs (right). Arthur's last companion – differently named in different versions; best known as Bedivere – stands in the perspectiveless distance. Reluctantly obedient, he has cast the weapon out over the water. A mysterious dweller below has caught it and will draw it under. Arthur, wounded, sits huddled on the ground (not even a chair; the trappings of royalty are gone) and awaits Bedivere's report. Excalibur, a magical token of his unique character, cannot remain after his passing. It must return to the realm of faerie. (French manuscript illustration, early 14th c.)

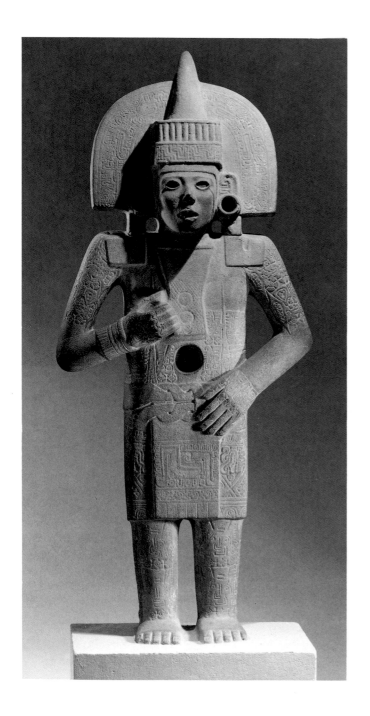

A Mexican god in human form. Pre-Columbian America had several myths about a divine culture-hero who ruled the primitive tribes, taught them laws and useful arts, and was then driven out, but, like Arthur, would return – either in person or by proxy through emissaries. In Mexico he was Quetzalcoatl (above), in Peru he was Viracocha. Similar figures in the countries between included the Mayan Itzamna and the Colombian Bochica. (Huastec limestone figure, Mexico, 900–1250.)

Kalki, Vishnu's tenth avatar (Krishna was the eighth). Hinduism teaches that the world has passed through phases or yugas, beginning with the glorious Krita Yuga and then declining. We are now in the fourth and worst. When lawlessness prevails everywhere, Vishnu will return as Kalki, destroying the evil and restoring the golden age. As destroyer, he will be a winged white horse; as restorer, a wise, powerful brahmin. The illustration combines human and equine imagery. (Indian miniature, Amber, c. 1720.)

Arthur in Avalon, imagined by a Victorian painter. He has drawn on Malory, who identifies four women headed by Morgan le Fay. He may also have consulted Geoffrey, who says Morgan applied her arts to heal Arthur's wound: she is holding a book. But this is the Somerset Avalon, Glastonbury, once a seaport. Willows mark the location, and the cowled figure is the Abbot. (*La Morte d'Arthur* by James Archer, *c*. 1861.)

Glastonbury Tor, the highest hill in the cluster where the town and Abbey now are. On the summit, archaeologists have revealed many centuries of occupation. The tower is all that remains of a church of St Michael. The hill is claimed as a sanctuary of pre-Christian religion. Around its sides are apparent traces of a septenary maze. Legends assert it to be hollow, a point of entry to the Otherworld. In recent years it has attracted neo-pagans and other seekers after 'alternative' spirituality.

Dante with his *Divine Comedy*. In the distance is the Mount of Purgatory, which he imagines on an island in the southern hemisphere. Departed souls are purified on its seven encircling terraces. The wooded summit is the Earthly Paradise; Dante suggests that golden-age myths are reminiscences of it. His conception defies Christian tradition, and even if his intentions are allegorical he has something other than *Genesis* in mind. A likely source, via Islam, is the paradisal Mount Meru of Indian cosmology. (Florentine painting, 16th c.)

A scene from the film *L'Éternel Retour* (1943), written by Jean Cocteau (right). His screenplay modernizes the Tristan legend. The lovers become Patrice, played by Jean Marais, and Natalie, played by Madeleine Sologne. By debasing some of the secondary characters, and inventing others equally unendearing, Cocteau establishes a contrast making the lovers' passion radically 'different', a recovery of glories lost in a sordid environment.

Awake! Awake Jerusalem! O lovely Emanation of Albion
Awake and overspread all Nations as in Ancient Time
For lo! the Night of Death is past and the Eternal Day
Appears upon our Hills: Awake Jerusalem, and come away

So spake the Vision of Albion & in him so spake in my hearing
The Universal Father. Then Albion stretchd his hand into Infinitude.
And took his Bow. Fourfold the Vision for bright beaming Urizen
Layd his hand on the South & took a breathing Bow of carved Gold
Luvah his hand stretchd to the East & bore a Silver Bow bright shining
Tharmas Westward a Bow of Brass pure flaming richly wrought
Urthona Northward in thick storms a Bow of Iron terrible thundering

And the Bow is a Male & Female & the Quiver of the Arrows of Love,
Are the Children of this Bow: a Bow of Mercy & Loving-kindness: laying
Open the hidden Heart in Wars of mutual Benevolence Wars of Love
And the Hand of Man grasps firm between the Male & Female Loves
And he Clothed himself in Bow & Arrows in awful state Fourfold
In the midst of his Twenty-eight Cities each with his Bow breathing

William Blake's picture of awakened Albion. For him the Arthurian legend reflects a greater reality. 'Albion' is an ancient name of Britain, and Blake's Albion is Britain personified. But he is more, because the poet adopts a theory that Britain was the universal fountain-head of wisdom and culture. All humanity was an extension of Albion, so Albion can represent all humanity. The world fell into degeneracy and strife, which Blake symbolizes as Albion sinking into a deathlike trance. The sleep of Arthur is an image of this in familiar legend. When Arthur wakes, 'the Sun of Britain shall rise again', and that corresponds to Albion's future waking. (Illustration from William Blake's *Jerusalem*, London, 1804).

Themes

King Arthur. German sculpture, possibly
from a group of the Nine Worthies,
13th c. Germanisches Nationalmuseum,
Nuremberg.

In all versions of his story Arthur brings order out of chaos, routing Saxon invaders, subduing regional tyrants, establishing the rule of law. He is supposedly the heir to a British crown worn by many kings descended from the Trojan Brutus, who founded the monarchy under the guidance of the goddess Diana. Soon after Britain's separation from Rome, Arthur revives its ancient glory.

As Geoffrey of Monmouth's royal messiah he has an authentic touch of Late Roman atmosphere. After a crisis in the third century AD the Empire was pulled together by Diocletian and Constantine. A mystique of world civilization surrounded it. When Constantine's father Constantius recovered a temporarily lost Britain, a medallion portrayed him as 'Restorer of

Medallion of the Emperor Constantius Chlorus with inscription *Redditor Lucis Aeternae*, c. AD 300. British Museum, London.

The Discovery of Arthur's Tomb. Drawing by John Hamilton Mortimer, c. 1767. National Galleries of Scotland, Edinburgh.

the Eternal Light' with London paying homage. During the subsequent decline, the hope of a *Restitutor Orbis*, a World-Restorer, who would expel barbarians, crush usurpers, and bring universal peace, was kept alive almost to the end. Arthur is a kind of *Restitutor* in an imperial successor-state.

After Geoffrey he was generally accepted as real. About 1190 the Glastonbury monks claimed to have found his grave, with an inscribed cross identifying the occupant. Archaeology offers nothing with his name on it, but shows that the monks did find an ancient grave, and that at three major Arthurian locations – Tintagel, Cadbury Castle, and Glastonbury itself – the story-tellers picked on places that were important at about the right time. Three correct guesses would be unlikely. For this reason and others, there is no doubt that historical tradition went into Arthur's making, and, incidentally, placed him in the period where the *Restitutor* motif genuinely belongs.

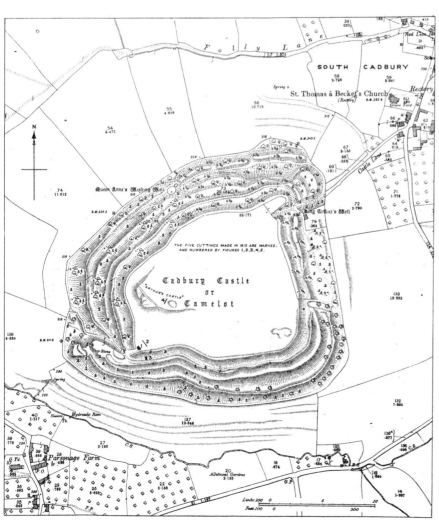

Brutus's voyage to Britain. Illustration from a genealogy produced in York, *c.* 1300. MS. Bodl. Rolls 3. Bodleian Library, Oxford.

Cadbury Castle or Camelot. Ordnance Survey plan.

Cross (now lost) unearthed at Glastonbury in 1190/91. The inscription reads: 'Here lies buried the renowned King Arthur in the Isle of Avalon.' After Camden's *Britannia*, 1607.

The wonderful child

Merlin and the child Arthur. Illustration by Gustave Doré to Tennyson's *Idylls of the King*, 1868.

Ygerna gives Arthur into the care of Sir Ector de Marys. Northern French manuscript illustration, 14th c. MS. Add. 10,292, f. 97v. British Library, London.

Adoration of the Magi. Detail of painting by Dosso Dossi, first half of 16th c. National Gallery, London.

Merlin knows from the outset that Arthur's destiny is special. Besides contriving his conception, the enchanter arranges for his mother to hand him over to Ector as foster-father, for a safe and secret upbringing. Tennyson, disliking Uther's scandalous exploit, invented – though without commitment – a still more remarkable origin, with Merlin seeing a luminous ship at night and finding the infant washed ashore at Tintagel.

For Christians the most important child of this kind is Jesus himself, whose coming is announced by an angel, and whom the Magi (probably astrologers) make a long journey to see and venerate, knowing him to be the expected Messiah.

In Tibetan Buddhism, the Dalai Lamas are successive manifestations of an immortal being. When a Dalai Lama dies, it is assumed that a new incarnation has occurred. Search parties look for male children born directly after the Lama's decease, and show the candidates certain sacred objects, believing that the correct one will give signs of recognition. Boys identified by this method have generally proved equal to the office. It is not in fact impossible to judge, or discern, that a small child will be outstanding.

A modern instance is Krishnamurti. A colleague of Annie Besant, head of the Theosophical Society, picked him out when he was very young and told her he would be the next World Teacher, in succession to Buddha and Christ. She adopted him and prepared him for his mission. As an adult he honourably refused it, yet he did become a spiritual teacher after his own fashion, with a distinguished reputation. The Theosophist who first noticed him was right in principle.

Krishnamurti. Illustration by Hamzeh Carr for *At the Feet of the Master*, 1926.

The fourteenth Dalai Lama, photographed in 1942.

Inspiration and paranormal powers

On Merlin as seer, royal adviser, and wonder-working sponsor of Arthur's reign, several traditions converge. He has some likeness to the Druids, who were magicians and counsellors to rulers. Behind the Druids is the ancient figure of the shaman, channel of messages from the gods. Asian shamanism is probably Druidism's remote ancestor, and it is thought to have been ancestral also to the cult of Apollo, who gave advice through his oracle at Delphi. Greek writers associated both Apollo and the Druids with people called Hyperboreans who were originally conceived as living in northern Asia, shamanic country.

The Welsh form of 'Merlin', i.e. 'Myrddin', is a sobriquet rather than a name. A Welsh text says Britain was formerly Myrddin's Precinct. This could look back to a deity, and if he was a god of inspiration, like Apollo, it would be apparent how an inspired seer could have been known as a Myrddin-man or simply a Myrddin. The word marks a connection with Carmarthen. Stonehenge's bluestones are believed to have been quarried in the Prescelly Mountains, not enormously far from there. A link with the god of a sacred area may explain why

Uther, Merlin and Ygerna. English manuscript illustration, 14th c. MS. Roy. 20.A.II, f. 3v. British Library, London.

Merlin re-erecting Stonehenge on Salisbury Plain. From a 14th c. French romance. MS. Egerton 3028, f. 30r. British Library, London.

Apollo at Delphi. Greek vase painting by the Kleophon painter, 5th c. BC. Museo Archeologico, Ferrara.

Merlin brings Stonehenge from the west
and sets it up: he has absorbed a myth of
this happening through the will and power
of the god, for whom, perhaps,
Stonehenge was a British Delphi. The
closest parallel to Merlin definitely is a
god, Krishna, who aids the heroes of the
Mahabharata and sustains their chief
warrior on the battlefield.

Like other characters from Celtic
antiquity, Merlin is medievalized in
romance. But the story of his being a
devil's son hints at a lingering awareness
that, although nominally Christian, he has
pre-Christian roots.

Shaman's mask. Tlingit, from Canada.
American Museum of Natural History,
New York.

Krishna as charioteer, with Prince Arjuna.
Detail of illustration from the
Mahabharata, 18th c. MS. Or. 13,180,
f. 8v. British Library, London.

Fragments of an older world

Fairy-folk too are found in Arthurian legend. While fairy lore is composite, notions about a pre-Celtic people, elusively surviving, went into it. Oberon, who becomes the fairies' king, is a son of Morgan le Fay.

Near Tintagel is a rock inscribed with an ancient septenary maze-spiral. The terraces around Glastonbury Tor may be remnants of a maze on this pattern. A story of Guinevere's abduction by the ruler of Somerset, her imprisonment at Glastonbury, and Arthur's rescue of her, may be related to tales of similar mazes in other contexts, where a hero makes his way to a woman at the centre. Indian legend parallels it in the story of Sita, Rama's wife, being imprisoned in Lanka.

Arthur and some of his knights, like Merlin, trail reminiscences of antiquity. They fight giants, for instance. Arthur himself meets two very alarming ones. According to Geoffrey, giants lived in Britain before the Trojans and gave them trouble when they arrived. Most were exterminated, but some survived in wild places and could have had descendants. Geoffrey mentions giants in several countries besides Britain. Their distribution suggests that they are megalith-builders, in and around the third millennium BC. Later generations supposed that the huge stone monuments could not have been raised by ordinary-sized people.

Monsters of mythology such as dragons are less prominent, but they occur. The conception of knights as dragon-slayers persists in Spenser's *Faerie Queene*. More puzzling are some other animal images, as in an Italian mosaic where Arthur is riding on a goat, with a medley of beasts, humans and signs of the Zodiac around him. A theory asserts that signs of the Zodiac are also marked out in the landscape of Somerset, forming the prototype of the Round Table.

Arthur fights the giant of Mont-Saint-Michel. Initial from a 12th c. copy of Geoffrey of Monmouth's *History*. MS. 880, f. 66v. Bibliothèque Municipale, Douai.

The Red Cross Knight slaying a dragon. Woodcut from Edmund Spenser's *Faerie Queene*, 1590.

King Arthur. Detail of mosaic floor in Otranto Cathedral, c. 1160.

Prince Henry as Oberon. Drawing by Inigo Jones, c. 1610. Trustees of the Chatsworth Settlement.

King Arthur's conjectured Round Table of the Zodiac, in Somerset.

Fortress Lanka depicted as a maze. From Alberuni's book on India, c. 1045.

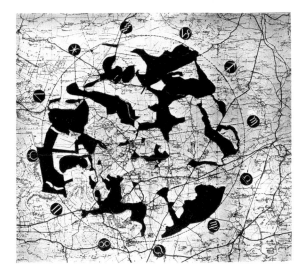

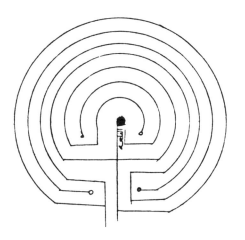

Imagery of greatness

Despite his complex antecedents, and his actual *floruit*, the Arthur of romance is a medieval monarch. The normal practice of updating puts him in the company of other heroes given the same treatment. It happens, for example, to all the Nine Worthies, not himself alone. As illustrated they are, from left to right: Hector, Caesar, Alexander, Joshua, David, Judas Maccabaeus, Arthur, Charlemagne, Godfrey. Arthur's standard is a personal emblem, and the crowns on it reappear in other pictures, sometimes, as here, in a set of three.

The Nine Worthies. French manuscript illustration, 14th c. Bibliothèque Nationale, Paris.

King Arthur and his kingdoms. Illustration from the *Chronicle* of Peter of Langtoft, 14th c. MS. Roy. 20.A.II, f. 4r. British Library, London.

King Arthur as warrior. Swiss woodcut, c. 1460–80. Burgerbibliothek, Bern.

Arthur has to be the greatest of rulers, and chroniclers itemizing his empire go far beyond Geoffrey, making him overlord of thirty countries, sometimes extending as far as Egypt. Such conquests imply supremacy as a warrior and war-leader. In peacetime he is a paragon of chivalry, presiding over the creation of knights and the conduct of tournaments. His wealth is vast and he is open-handed with it, spending it not only on general magnificence but on the relief of subjects' distress, and holding banquets where noble guests are made welcome.

Tristan fighting in a tournament. French manuscript illustration, 1463. MS. Fr. 99, f. 561r. Bibliothèque Nationale, Paris.

Lancelot relating his adventures. French manuscript illustration, c. 1316. MS. Roy. 14.E.III, f. 89. British Library, London.

William Bruges, first Garter King of Arms, kneeling before St George. English manuscript illustration, c. 1430. MS. Stowe 594, f. 5v. British Library, London.

Edward III in Garter robes. English manuscript illustration, c. 1430. MS. Stowe 594, f. 7v. British Library, London.

Jean II and Knights of the Star. French manuscript illustration, 14th c. MS. Fr. 2813, f. 394. Bibliothèque Nationale, Paris.

Early Welsh tradition presents Arthur as the head of a band of warriors. It has been conjectured that his original defeated the Saxons by forming a corps of cavalry on the Late Roman model. When he is taken up in medieval literature, his companions do reappear as knights — horsemen, *chevaliers* — and in romance they become the Knights of the Round Table, vowed to the code of chivalry, with social and religious responsibilities. A knight was supposed to be brave, loyal, courteous, proficient in arms. He righted wrongs and succoured the weak. Real orders of knighthood were often closely affiliated to the Church, and had celestial patrons such as St George.

Kings and nobles in England, who took Arthur very seriously, held entertainments called Round Tables at which the guests impersonated Arthurian characters, feasted and jousted. In 1344 Edward III considered refounding the Round Table as an actual order, though, in the end, he founded the Order of the Garter instead. Jean II of France had similar interests. A fourteenth-century French companionship, the Knights of the Star, was launched as an explicit successor to Arthur's. The Order of St Patrick was a belated Irish equivalent for the Garter, instituted when Ireland was under the British crown.

Reverberations continued into times when orders of chivalry were somewhat devalued. In 1721 a club was formed in London styled the Knights of the Round Table, but its members were not knights, they were mostly actors. Frederick, Prince of Wales, attended meetings; he enjoyed amateur theatricals. As the Honourable Society of Knights of the Round Table it still exists. Its membership now is largely military and naval. It was represented on the Camelot Research Committee which excavated Cadbury Castle in 1966–70.

Table of Honour of Knights of the Star. French manuscript illustration, 14th c. MS. Fr. 2813, f. 394. Bibliothèque Nationale, Paris.

Installation Banquet of the Knights of St Patrick. Painting by John Keyse Sherwin, 1783. National Gallery of Ireland, Dublin.

Women

Behind Guinevere are traditions of Celtic
queens. Behind Morgan le Fay, and the
Lady of the Lake, are traditions of
priestesses and goddesses.

A Celtic queen could reign in her own
right, lead armies as Boudicca did, take
lovers as Cartimandua did in northern
Britain. To medieval authors such free and
equal women were unacceptable, even
incomprehensible. Not only is Guinevere
regarded as forward and unfaithful, she is
always defined in relation to a man, to her
husband or lover, even when she is
portrayed (as she sometimes is) with a
certain sympathy. Likewise, since pagan
myth and magic are now suspect or
worse, Morgan becomes a witch
scheming against Arthur, the Lake-Damsel
Nimue becomes the ruin of a besotted
Merlin.

William Blake, for whom these legends
echo the greater reality of Albion, is
ambivalent towards women. He speaks
scathingly of a corrupt 'female will', with
Arthur as well as Merlin falling victim to it.
But things should be otherwise, and they
can be. His poem *Visions of the Daughters
of Albion* looks towards women's sexual
liberty, without prudery or possessiveness.

Marion Zimmer Bradley, in her
Arthurian novel *The Mists of Avalon*,
seeks to re-create the true feminine
element through a fresh appraisal of
Morgan.

Boudicca. Sculpture by Thomas
Thornycroft, erected on the Thames
Embankment 1902.

The Beguiling of Merlin. Painting by Sir
Edward Burne-Jones, 1874. Walker Art
Gallery, Liverpool.

Lancelot and Guinevere played by
Nicholas Clay and Cherie Lunghi in the
film *Excalibur*, 1981.

Title page of *Visions of the Daughters of
Albion* by William Blake, 1793.

The Mists of Avalon by Marion Bradley.
Cover illustration by Brad Bradlt, 1984.

Golden ages

The Golden Age. Painting by Lucas Cranach (1472–1553). Nasjonalgalleriet, Oslo.

The Court of Pan. Painting by Luca Signorelli, 1478. Formerly Kaiser Friedrich Museum, Berlin (destroyed).

Timur Enthroned with His Descendants. Mughal miniature by Hashim, *c*. 1650. India Office Library, London.

While Arthur's medieval guise is the most familiar, and the one he has in most of the literature, he is a shape-shifter. He has been in succession the patriotic leader of Celtic Britain, the focus of Welsh heroic saga, the empire-builder of Geoffrey, the lord of a chivalric Utopia, the Tennysonian idealist. His legend's repeated fading-out and revival show a

vitality best explained by a feature that persists throughout, its appeal to the multiform daydream of a past golden age.

This has fastened on other national heroes, if less fruitfully. As a general notion it need not look back immensely far. Thus, industrialized societies can breed a nostalgia inspired by fantasies of idyllic rural life, not very long ago; a nostalgia that can be exploited. Usually, however, the golden age is remote enough to blur any real sense of chronology.

Its psychological basis is a vague sense of 'Paradise lost'. This cannot, in itself, project specific golden ages like Arthur's, but it can influence the shape taken by legends and history as imagination reshapes them at different times. It has conjured up eras of carefree innocence and idealized paganism, and imposed astonishing fancies on real antiquity, suggesting, for instance, that Stonehenge was the open-air temple of a pastoral Arcadia.

Idealized Russian village scene. Detail of Soviet record sleeve of *Russian Folk Chorus* by Piatnitsky, 1950.

Stonehenge in Arcadia. Detail of painting by Thomas Cole, *The Arcadian or Pastoral State*, 1836. The New-York Historical Society.

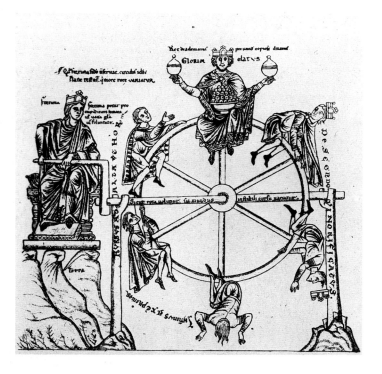

The Expulsion from Eden. Detail of manuscript illustration from *Les Très Riches Heures du Duc de Berry*, f. 25v., by the Limbourg brothers, c. 1411. Musée Condé, Chantilly.

The Wheel of Fortune from the *Hortus deliciarum* of Herrad of Landsberg. Facsimile of 12th c. original (destroyed).

The Fall of the Titans. Roman sarcophagus, 2nd c. AD. Vatican Museums, Rome.

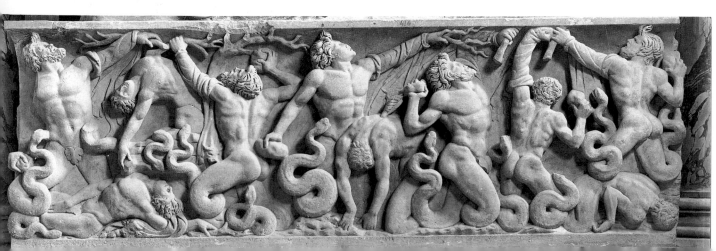

Mutability and downfall

Medieval minds could conceive a Utopia, and such was the regime of Arthur. Yet there would always be qualifications. One of the first Lancelot romances, set early in the reign, portrays the King himself as unjust and oppressive; he has an ominous dream, a mysterious visitor upbraids him, and henceforth he is a reformed character. Generally of course romancers treat his reign as good.

But Christian writers could never wholly forget Christian doctrine. All golden ages had an apparent prototype, humanity's pristine happiness in the Earthly Paradise of Eden. Our first parents sinned and were driven out, into a world foreordained to toil, grief, mortality. For orthodox Christians the Fall was a fact of life, and while Christ gave the means of spiritual survival, the world did not alter fundamentally. There could be good times, but they could not be expected to last.

In medieval thinking, mutability applies to individuals too, including the greatest, even when, at their best, they create good times themselves. Fortune turns her wheel bringing the fall of princes. The *Alliterative Morte Arthure* tells of the King's imperial ambition soaring too high, and of a warning dream in which he sees the wheel raising and lowering the Nine Worthies, himself among them. This is simply a way of saying what the whole Arthurian cycle says, that the glory of Arthur is doomed, sapped from within.

Christianity points up what many non-Christian minds are aware of. The golden age of Greek myth was ruled by the Titans under Cronus, and ended in decline and mortality when the Titans fell. In the Arcadia of poetic fancy, Death is still present. Paul Gauguin's art evokes a Pacific paradise of innocence, yet he sees corruption creeping in.

Shepherds in Arcady. Painting by Nicolas Poussin, c. 1630. Trustees of the Chatsworth Settlement.

Vaïraumati tei oa (Paradise Corrupted). Painting by Paul Gauguin, 1892. Pushkin Museum, Moscow.

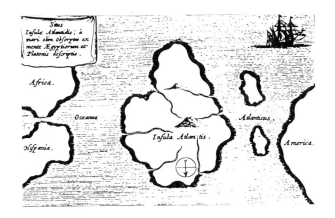

Isles of the Blest

When Arthur is borne away over water, accompanied by women and bound for Avalon, he fades into immemorial myth. Plutarch records the British belief about a beautiful western island with a cave where a banished god lay asleep. This is in the background of stories of Arthur's departure and immortality, on an island or in a cave. Plutarch interweaves it with other notions of trans-oceanic lands, the most famous being Plato's Atlantis. Whatever sources the classical authors used, there is no doubt about the Celts' Atlantic mythology. It appears at its richest in Irish tales telling of dozens of islands, one being the apple-isle Emain Ablach. Avalon – in Welsh, Avallach – is originally the same.

Legendary Irish seafarers wander in this vast archipelago. The hint for their adventures came from a technological fact, the invention of the curragh, an efficient sea-going craft in which Irishmen actually did reach the Faeroes and Iceland. Some of the mythic islands are dangerous, but some are idyllic, 'without grief, without sorrow, without death'. One of the idyllic kind is the Land of Women. The women who receive Arthur belong to the same fairy-world, probably once a goddess-world.

The very popular *Voyage of St Brendan* follows his quest for the 'Land Promised to the Saints' where the Earthly Paradise is. Barinthus, a westward seafarer whose report inspires Brendan's quest, reappears as the pilot in Geoffrey's version of the Avalon voyage. Brendan's reputed discoveries influenced medieval map-makers, and also Columbus, whose own discoveries were given mythical qualities.

Map showing Atlantis. From Athanasius Kircher's *Mundus subterraneus*, 1678.

The voyage of St Brendan. German manuscript illustration, 15th c. Cod. Pal. Germ. 60, f. 159r. Universitätsbibliothek, Heidelberg.

Arrival of Columbus in America. Detail of engraving from Théodore de Bry's *America*, 1594.

In China, Taoist alchemists believed in an island-paradise where immortal sages dwelt. They even sailed out into the Pacific in search of it. Romanticization of real Pacific islands began in the eighteenth century, and is still apparent in the paintings of Gauguin, who may be said to have created his own Land of Women.

The Taoist paradise. Chinese carved lacquer panel inset with jade, lapis lazuli and gilt metal, 18th c. Victoria & Albert Museum, London.

Te nave nave fenua (Delicious Land). Painting by Paul Gauguin, 1892. Ohara Museum of Art, Kurashiki.

Charlemagne. Painting by Albrecht Dürer, 1512. Germanisches Nationalmuseum, Nuremberg.

Barbarossa in the Kyffhäuser. Detail of drawing by Robert Müller (1815–1854). National-Galerie, Staatliche Museen, Berlin.

Napoleon rising from the grave. Engraving after Horace Vernet, c. 1840. Bibliothèque Nationale, Paris.

Survival of apparent death, and expected return, is a theme with variations. Charlemagne died in 814 and was entombed at Aachen. Yet it was foretold in the Middle Ages that he would come back to life and lead the crusaders, or that a Second Charlemagne, somehow re-embodying him, would establish world-wide justice and peace.

The German emperor Frederick was the subject of a belief resembling Arthur's cave legend, and very likely inspired by it. This applied originally to Frederick II, later to Frederick I, Barbarossa. From the fifteenth century on he was said to be asleep in a secret chamber inside a mountain, the Kyffhäuser. One day he would wake and reign in glory over the German nation.

Napoleon, who died in 1821, could not return literally. But the reinterment of his ashes in Paris was a kind of return, and reinforced a growing mystique. His symbolic resurrection helped his nephew to sweep to power as Napoleon III.

President Kennedy, posthumously an American Arthur-figure, was rumoured during the 1970s to be still alive, though comatose through brain damage. The story had the duality of Arthur's. He was

President J.F. Kennedy. Detail of Norman Rockwell's painting *A Time for Greatness* for the cover of *Look*, July 1964.

Ezekiel's vision. Initial from the Winchester Bible, f. 172r., 12th c. Cathedral Library, Winchester.

housed with his life-support machine either in a sealed-off floor of a Dallas hospital, the equivalent of Arthur's cave, or on a Greek island, the equivalent of Avalon.

A science-fiction variant is the theory of Erich von Däniken, according to which superior beings from other worlds visited this one long ago, and they, or their descendants, will be back some day for humanity's benefit. They have made reconnaissance trips already. The visionary chariot of *Ezekiel* 1:4–28 was a spaceship.

The mystique of restoration

Prince Arthur. Anonymous painting,
16th c. Windsor Castle.

The Emperor Augustus. Onyx cameo,
1st c. AD. Kunsthistorisches Museum,
Vienna.

Hussite Sermon. Painting by Carl
Friedrich Lessing, 1836. Kunstmuseum,
Düsseldorf.

Psychologically the Great Return does not depend on literal belief in legends, or even in particular individuals. Henry VII's exploitation of Arthurian prophecy could dispense with Arthur himself. He traced his own ancestry to early Welsh kings, and marched to overthrow Richard III flying a Red Dragon standard. His professed restoration of the 'British' monarchy was to be completed by the son whom he named Arthur and had baptized at Winchester, Malory's Camelot. This prospective Arthur II died young and was never king; yet the Tudor myth could dispense with him too, and lasted till the end of the dynasty.

The theme of Arthur's reign, departure and return gives mythic shape to a phenomenon with wider bearings. Not only does the idea of a lost golden age take numerous forms, there is often a readiness to believe that it is not lost for ever, that it can be reinstated, and that this is a proper aim in the real world.

Virgil hails the rule of Augustus as leading to a rebirth of the *Saturnia regna*, the golden time that flourished under Cronus or Saturn. Christian reformers in the later Middle Ages, and their successors both Catholic and Protestant, sought to combat a corrupt ecclesiastical system by bringing back the Christianity of the primitive Church. Gandhi mobilized the Indian masses under the British Raj by speaking of an ideal ancient India of village communes and cottage industries, and teaching millions to use the spinning-wheel as a living revival of it. The state of Israel came into being because of prolonged Zionist insistence that the destiny of the Jewish people demanded an ingathering to the Promised Land, the long-lost, long-desired home, and that no other haven from persecution would do.

On the Way to Zion. Painting by Isaac Levitan, late 19th c. Israel Museum, Jerusalem.

Mahatma Gandhi at his spinning-wheel at the Harijan Colony, Delhi, 1940.

Victoria's Arthur

After Elizabeth I, the Arthurian legend slid into a phase of decline. Milton considered it but wrote *Paradise Lost* instead. Dryden confined himself to an opera, notable only for Purcell's music. Then Sir Richard Blackmore perpetrated two epics of such prodigious badness that the theme was discredited.

It revived in the nineteenth century. Tennyson was not its first rehandler, but he was easily the most influential, and, at his best, very good indeed. After some early medium-length treatments he wrote the *Idylls of the King*, dedicated to the memory of Prince Albert, and conceived in reverence for the royal widow and her values. In his hands the legend retained its medieval form, but expressed contemporary ideals and ethics. He was popular as few poets are, a genuine best-seller. Other poets took up the Matter of Britain, and so did artists.

At Tennyson's invitation a photographer, Julia Margaret Cameron, illustrated the *Idylls* using a medley of models, including her husband and her gardener. The Pre-Raphaelites produced Arthurian murals and canvases. Emphasis shifted somewhat. Galahad, as a pure-hearted, spiritually directed hero, became more prominent than he was in the Middle Ages.

Tennysonian morality provoked reactions, from Swinburne for instance. Beardsley's illustrations to Malory conjure up a rather different atmosphere. Mark Twain's *A Connecticut Yankee in King Arthur's Court* makes fun of the whole business, though with a curious ambiguity. Most of the story debunks romantic medievalism, implying that the modern man is superior to Arthur's people, yet in the end his misuse of technological know-how for mass killing shows him to be actually worse.

King Arthur. Photograph by Julia Margaret Cameron for Tennyson's *Idylls of the King*, 1874. Royal Photographic Society, Bath.

Sir Galahad. Painting by Arthur Hughes, 1870. Walker Art Gallery, Liverpool.

The Arming and Departure of the Knights of the Round Table on the Quest of the Holy Grail. Tapestry after a design by Sir Edward Burne-Jones, *c*. 1890. City Museum and Art Gallery, Birmingham.

Sir Lancelot caricatured. Illustration by Daniel Beard to Mark Twain's *A Connecticut Yankee in King Arthur's Court*, 1889.

Morgan le Fay and Tristan. Illustration by Aubrey Beardsley to Malory's *Le Morte d'Arthur*, 1893–94.

HOW. MORGAN.LE FAY.GAVE.A.SHIELD. TO.SIR.TRISTRAM.

Tristan and Isolde sailing to Cornwall.
French manuscript illustration, *c.* 1410.
Cod. 2537, f. 50. Österreichische
Nationalbibliothek, Vienna.

Tristan and Isolde. Painting by John
Duncan, 1912. City Art Centre,
Edinburgh.

Parsifal. Stage design by Paul von
Joukovsky, for the closing scene of Act III
of Wagner's opera, Bayreuth, 1882.
Richard Wagner Gedenkstätte, Bayreuth.

Music-drama

Arthurian subjects have had many theatrical treatments, but few or none have been in the first rank. Operatic versions are dominated by three music-dramas of Richard Wagner. After the marginally Arthurian *Lohengrin* came *Tristan und Isolde*, based on a medieval romance by Gottfried von Strassburg. Wagner simplifies the plot and centres it firmly on the couple's tragic and transfiguring love, due to their mistakenly drinking a potion while at sea. *Parsifal*, on the Grail theme, is derived from Wolfram von Eschenbach's epic *Parzival*, itself derived partly from the romance of Perceval by Chrétien de Troyes. But the half-pagan atmosphere of Perceval's experience is entirely Christianized.

Among English composers, Arthur Sullivan, who had ambitions beyond his collaboration with Gilbert, attempted an Arthurian opera but abandoned it. Only fragments survive. Rutland Boughton, best known for *The Immortal Hour* and the choral work *Bethlehem*, had larger ideas. Supported by Bernard Shaw and other notables, he launched the Glastonbury Festival in 1914 and continued it through the post-war decade, with the goal of making the legendary place an English Bayreuth. While the Festival had some success, his own cycle of Arthurian operas lacked lustre and has never been performed in its entirety. It has the odd distinction of being the only version that ends with a peasants' revolt.

Tristan und Isolde. Setting for Act III of Wieland Wagner's production of Wagner's opera, Bayreuth, 1966.

Parsifal. The Grail Temple scene in Wieland Wagner's production of Wagner's opera, Bayreuth, 1971.

Transitions

A modern Arthurian development has
been the growth of a 'New Matter of
Britain'. Novelists such as Rosemary
Sutcliff and Persia Woolley, while
respecting the medieval versions and
drawing on them, have gone back beyond
to imagine Post-Roman Britain as it might
actually have been, or (as in the case of
Marion Bradley) to use it as a matrix for
their own myth-making. In the visual
media, however, this trend has been
unproductive, apart from a television
series called *Arthur of the Britons*, aimed
at junior viewers. It is assumed that only

the romance-world, or something akin to it, can be made acceptable to a wide public.

The musical *Camelot* is in substance T.H. White, except for its portrayal of Mordred as a sneering iconoclast, and the film version keeps and increases the medieval splendour. Robert Bresson's film *Lancelot du Lac* is a sombre study of the old triangle, Arthur–Guinevere–Lancelot. Bresson, strangely, has the King and his knights wearing full armour most of the time. This hyper-medieval invention reappears in John Boorman's *Excalibur*,

which, though founded on Malory, mixes its imagery to detach the action from any definite period – as indeed Bresson does to a slight extent. Boorman's film also has an echo of White, in its introduction of Arthur first as a boy. Merlin, however, is more interesting, a powerful ambivalent figure between the Druidic and Christian worlds, as a real Merlin might have been.

A series of British stamps showed that the pictorial Arthur was still the medieval one, and that the novelists of the New Matter had yet to make any impression visually.

Camelot. 1967 film with David Hemmings as Mordred.

Excalibur. 1981 film with Nigel Terry as Arthur.

Lancelot du Lac. 1974 film with Luc Simon and Laura Duke Condominas as Lancelot and Guinevere.

Excalibur. 1981 film with Nicol Williamson as Merlin.

Set of British postage stamps with figures from Arthurian legend. Issued 1986.

SOURCES AND FURTHER READING

TEXTS

Alliterative Morte Arthure. See Wilhelm (1).

Chrétien de Troyes. See Wilhelm (1) and (2).

Culhwch and Olwen. See *Mabinogion* and Wilhelm (1).

Geoffrey of Monmouth:
(1) *The History of the Kings of Britain*, trans., with introduction, by Lewis Thorpe, Penguin, Harmondsworth and New York 1966.
(2) *Vita Merlini*: The Life of Merlin, ed. and trans. J.J. Parry, University of Illinois Press, Urbana 1925.

Gildas, *De Excidio Britanniae*, ed. and trans. under the title *The Ruin of Britain* by Michael Winterbottom, in *History from the Sources*, vol. 7, Phillimore, Chichester 1978.

Layamon. See Wilhelm (2).

The Mabinogion, trans., with introduction, by Gwyn and Thomas Jones, Dent, London 1949; Dutton, New York 1949.

Malory, Sir Thomas, *Le Morte d'Arthur*: Caxton's text with modernized spelling, ed. Janet Cowan with introduction by John Lawlor, 2 vols., Penguin, Harmondsworth 1969 and New York 1970.

Mort Artu, trans. by James Cable as *The Death of King Arthur*, Penguin, Harmondsworth and New York 1971.

'Nennius', *Historia Brittonum*, ed. and trans. under the title *British History* by John Morris, in *History from the Sources*, vol. 8, Phillimore, Chichester 1980.

Queste del Saint Graal, trans. by P.M. Matarasso as *The Quest of the Holy Grail*, Penguin, Harmondsworth and New York 1969.

Sir Gawain and the Green Knight. See Wilhelm (1).

Tennyson, Alfred Lord, *Idylls of the King*. In *The Poems of Tennyson*, ed. Christopher Ricks, Longman, London 1969.

Wace. See Wilhelm (2).

White, T.H., *The Once and Future King*, Collins, London 1958.

Wilhelm, James J.:
(1) . . . and Laila Zamuelis Gross, eds., *The Romance of Arthur*, Garland, New York 1984. Includes *Culhwch and Olwen*, Chrétien's *Lancelot*, *Sir Gawain and the Green Knight*, and the *Alliterative Morte Arthure*, translated by several hands.
(2) ed., *The Romance of Arthur II*, Garland, New York 1986. Includes Chrétien's *Yvain*, and excerpts from Wace, Layamon, and romances of Merlin, translated by several hands.

Wolfram von Eschenbach, *Parzival*, trans. by A.T. Hatto, Penguin, Harmondsworth and New York 1980.

DISCUSSION AND CRITICISM

This list is, necessarily, highly selective. For additional works consult the bibliographies in Norris J. Lacy's *Arthurian Encyclopedia*.

Alcock, Leslie, *Arthur's Britain*, Allan Lane, The Penguin Press, London 1971; St Martin's Press, New York 1972.

Ashe, Geoffrey:
(1) *Avalonian Quest*, Methuen, London 1982.
(2) *Camelot and the Vision of Albion*, Heinemann, London 1971; St Martin's Press, New York 1972.
(3) *The Discovery of King Arthur*, Doubleday, New York 1985; Debrett, London 1985.
(4) *Land to the West*, Collins, London 1962; Viking, New York 1962.

Campbell, James, ed., *The Anglo-Saxons*, Phaidon, Oxford 1982; Cornell University Press, Ithaca (N.Y.) 1982.

Carley, James P., *Glastonbury Abbey*, Boydell, Woodbridge (Suffolk) 1988.

Eckhardt, Caroline D., 'Prophecy and Nostalgia': in *The Arthurian Tradition*, eds. M.F. Braswell and J. Bugge, University of Alabama Press, Tuscaloosa 1988.

Lacy, Norris J., ed., *The Arthurian Encyclopedia*, Garland, New York 1986; Boydell, Woodbridge (Suffolk) 1988.

Loomis, Roger Sherman, ed., *Arthurian Literature in the Middle Ages*, Clarendon Press, Oxford 1959.

Tolstoy, Nikolai, *The Quest for Merlin*, Hamish Hamilton, London 1985; Little, Brown, Boston 1985.

Westwood, Jennifer, *Albion: a Guide to Legendary Britain*, Granada, London and New York 1985.

ACKNOWLEDGMENTS

The objects and illustrations reproduced in the text and plates (pp. 6–64) are in the following collections:

Brussels, Bibliothèque Royale Albert Ier 36–37 (MS. 9243, f. 36v.). Musée de Chatillon sur Seine 50. Greenwich, National Maritime Museum 52. The Hague, Koninklijke Bibliotheek 56–57 (MS. KA XX, f. 163v.). London, British Library 19 (MS. Add. 10,294, f. 52), 40 (MS. Add. 34,294, f. 186v.), 42 (MS. Add. 18,850, f. 138), 46 above (MS. Or. 13,180, f. 149r.), 57 below (MS. Add. 10,294, f. 94); British Museum 16, 38; India Office Library 58–59; Lambeth Palace Library 41 (MS. 6, f. 62v.), 46 below (MS. 6, f. 43v.), 55 (MS. 6, f. 66v.); National Gallery 54; Victoria & Albert Museum 53. Manchester, City Art Galleries 60; John Rylands University Library 21 (Fr. MS. 1, f. 254r.). Munich, Bayerische Staatsbibliothek 27 (Cod. lat. 14,731, f. 82v.). New York, Brooklyn Museum 58; The Metropolitan Museum of Art 33. Oxford, Bodleian Library 6 (MS. Douce 178, f. 181v.), 35 (MS. Douce 383, f. 12v.). Paris, Bibliothèque de l'Arsenal 48 (MS. Fr. 3479, f. 1); Bibliothèque Nationale 34 (MS. Fr. 95, f. 159v.), 45 (MS. Fr. 99, f. 563), 49 (MS. Fr. 118, f. 219v.); Musée du Louvre 44. Vienna, Österreichische Nationalbibliothek 39 (Codex 2537, f. 26), 43 (Codex 2537, f. 233). Washington, National Gallery of Art 62

Sources of photographs:

Reproduced by Gracious Permission of Her Majesty the Queen 88 l; British Tourist Authority 78 above; E.C.F. Illustrations 15; Festspielleitung, Bayreuth 93 above and below; K.E. Maltwood, *King Arthur's Round Table of the Zodiac* (Victoria 1946) 73 centre r.; Mansell Collection 73 above r., 89 below; Lynn Muir 61; National Film Archive 47, 63, 94 above l., above r. and below l., 95 above; The Royal Photographic Society 51; Sotheby Parke Bernet Publications 73 l., The Warburg Institute 87 below.